I0162515

BLOWING UP THE NAZIS

WHAT YOU DIDN'T KNOW WILL BLOW YOUR MIND

ELLIOTT L. WATSON

Published by New Spur Publishing

First published 2018

Websites
www.versushistory.com

Twitter:
@VersusHistory
@thelibrarian6

Instagram:
versushistory

For inquiring minds and superheroes.
For Lala, Lucas, and Chicken.

FOREWORD

The genesis of this book is to be found somewhere in the latter months of 2017. More specifically, it was conceived by a question which was, in itself, born out of a frustration. The question, harmless enough, was from a student and it went something like this: "Why do we have to study the Nazis, again?". The question, to be sure, was a valid one. Why do students around the world, have to study the Nazis? The simple but inadequate answer is always, "Because it's important that we remember how these things can and do happen…". The retort from the student was plaintive, "But we've studied it so often that we already know everything about the Nazis. Can't we study something else? Please?". Irrespective of the rationale behind the inclusion of Nazi Germany on curricula across the planet's schools (although it seems profoundly necessary to my mind – particularly with anti-Semitism reportedly on the rise across the world), a more specific question began to burrow its way into my mind: "Do we really know everything about this subject?" Of course, the answer to this question, is "patently not". How could we? Nonetheless, the question nestled itself where it had settled in my mind and gestated. I began to wonder how much could a subject that I have taught for nearly twenty years, still have left for me to discover? The answer, as it turns out (and I should have known), was 'a lot'.

Partly in an attempt to satisfy my own curiosity and partly as a means of formulating a more well-informed response to students who might venture the same question as raised above, I determined to find some rarer, more surprising, elements of Nazi Germany. Perhaps, more importantly, I hoped to find some startling details of history that teachers could incorporate into their teaching to make it less, well, routine. This would serve two purposes: 1) it would engage students 2) it would cut the question of 'why we study Nazi Germany' off at the root, thus negating the need for it in the first instance. Well, that was the idea. And so, I set about researching for this book. It turns out that many of the pieces of history that can be found within these pages, were hidden in plain sight. Having said this, some were more difficult to uncover.

One decision I had to make early on in the writing was how to avoid boring the reader. Hopefully, the very nature of the content will go some way to solving that particular problem. Nevertheless, I thought it was important to write the book in such a way that it is accessible to all readers - not just academics or people who maintain a certain, dedicated, level of interest in the subject. Consequently, I have, where possible reduced the number of footnotes/endnotes, except for where they were absolutely necessary, and used an inclusive language. History, as far as I am concerned, should attempt to accomplish a number of goals that are noble, functional, accurate and honest. I also believe wholeheartedly that history should be presented, as far as is possible, in an interesting form. To this end, I have broken each chapter into four sub-headings: ***What you need to know; Why it's important that you know this; What this is connected to; What you didn't know will blow your mind.***

Too many students around the world are seeing the subject of History at school as more and more of a chore and, dare I say it, in the face of the demands of a technological revolution, an unnecessary subject. There should be no shame in trying to repopularise history. This book is my small contribution in this direction.

Many thanks to Dr Carrie Gibson for her kind words and encouragement. Thanks also to John Jackson who so generously agreed to let me use his fabulous photograph of the Washington County Courthouse in Ohio with the swastika-patterned floor. Special thanks to Patrick O'Shaughnessy, my Co-Editor at Versus History and all-round bow-tied legend.

Onwards.

Dr. Elliott L. Watson

CONTENTS

1

AKTION T4 AND THE BABY WHOSE DEATH STARTED A GENOCIDE

WHAT YOU NEED TO KNOW

There once stood a neo-classical building at Tiergartenstrasse 4, in the Berlin district of Tiergarten. This building no longer exists but at one time it housed *Zentraldienststelle-T4*, or the Central Office-T4. Later, at the Nuremberg Trials, the term ***Aktion T4*** (named for the 'actions' resulting from decisions taken at the address of this building) would become synonymous with some of the most heinous deeds carried out by the Nazis.

Gerhard Kretschmar was born on the 20th February 1939 to parents Richard and Lina, who were ardent Nazi loyalists. The baby Gerhard was born blind, with one arm, either one leg or no legs (reports vary since medical documents relating to the child have been lost or destroyed) and endured repeated convulsions. Richard Kretschmar took his son to the University Children's Clinic in Leipzig in the hope that he could be 'put to sleep'. Euthanasia was illegal in Germany and the attending physician - one Dr Werner Catel - told the father he was unable to carry out his wishes. What Richard Kretschmar did next set off a chain of events which, in the eyes of many, helped lead to the deaths of hundreds of thousands, if not millions, of people. He wrote to the Führer for a special dispensation to have 'this monster' (Kretschmar's words) euthanised.

The letter found its way to the desk of Hitler, most likely by route of Philipp Bouhler - head of his private secretariat - who was well aware of Hitler's proclivities in the direction of euthanasia, which he often called *gnadentod*. Roughly translated, gnadentod means 'mercy death'. Hitler ordered his private physician - one Karl Brandt - to head to Leipzig carrying instructions that, should his appraisal of the baby be as described by its father then, regardless of legality, it should be euthanised. Gerhard Kretschmar died on the 25th July 1939, most likely by a lethal injection of luminal. The child was buried three days later.

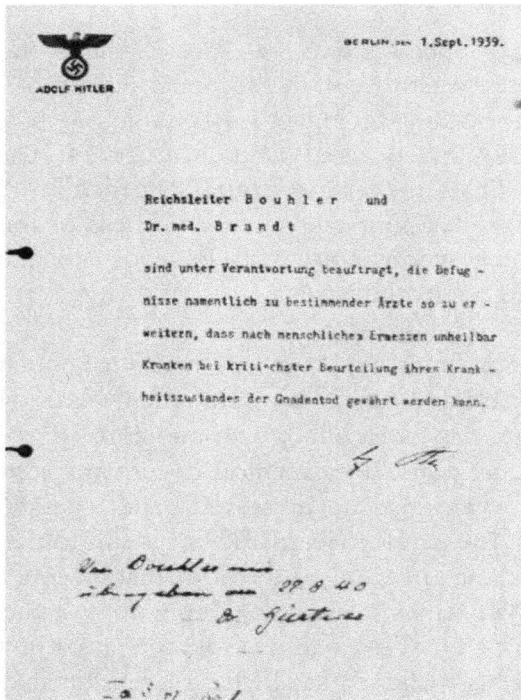

Picture 1: Hitler's directive authorising the euthanasia programme

The precedent had been set in the death of this unfortunate child. In October 1939, Hitler signed a directive which authorised, "Reichsleiter Bouhler and Dr Brandt...to be professionally accountable in charge to extend the legal authority of specific named Medical Doctors, so that they may grant euthanasia to...incurably sick patients..." (see *Picture 1*). This note was backdated to September 1st, the day the Nazis invaded Poland. Although a state secret, from September onwards Brandt and Bouhler organised a nationwide (and, not much later, an international) programme of involuntary euthanasia which murdered hundreds of thousands of people deemed 'unfit' for existence. Much of this programme was planned and coordinated from the neoclassical building at Tiergartenstrasse 4. The Programme was known as T4 by those involved. It became known as *Aktion T4* during the Nuremberg Trials after the defeat of the Nazis.

WHY IT'S IMPORTANT THAT YOU KNOW THIS

Hitler had 'dipped his toe' into the waters of genetic hygiene back in 1933 with the July 14th *Law for the Prevention of Progeny with Hereditary Diseases*. Under this law, close to 400,000 people adjudged to have hereditary illnesses were forcibly sterilised. Vague diagnoses cast a deliberately wide net in order to entrap those whom Hitler and the Nazis wished to purge from the gene pool of Germany. 'Feeblemindedness' was a common pronouncement, among others, by those medical personnel charged with applying the law. Although this law was not specifically racial in character - it served to 'clean' the pool rather than drain it - it would often be used to sterilise Gypsies, homosexuals, and other 'asocials'.

It doesn't require the most powerful of magnifying glasses to see the connective tissue between the ligaments of sterilisation and euthanasia. Hitler had expended great energies justifying the weaknesses of Germany in terms of the feeble elements within its population procreating at the expense of the stronger.

In Chapter XI of Mein Kampf, *Race and People*, Hitler claims that these weaker,

> "...hybrids and their progeny are denied the ordinary powers of resistance to disease or the natural means of defence against outer attack...and the final consequence would be that the best in quality would be forced to recede into the background. Therefore a corrective measure in favour of the better quality must intervene..."[1]. (MK p.222-223)

Sterilisation was the first step in the direction of this 'corrective measure'. However, although to modern sensibilities, forced sterilisation is largely repugnant, it *was* a generally accepted scientific and social model in many parts of the world at the time (see the American sterilisation programme in the final section of this chapter, below). And so, despite our contemporary distaste for forced sterilisation, it was not at all uncommon in the early twentieth century world. In many countries, including Germany, America, Britain, and Canada, it was in fact legal. Unfortunately, for Hitler euthanasia was not. That was, however, until the death of Gerhard Kretschmar - the baby whose father had written to the Führer in 1939.

There is very little doubt that Hitler's direct intervention in the euthanasia of the Kretschmar child was more than a simple act in line with his view of genetic health; it was, in the minds of many historians, a 'testing of the waters' to gauge the response of the medical profession and, should they find out, the general population. The former barely resisted and the latter didn't find out until much too late. The 'Kretschmar test case' was the second step towards Hitler's 'corrective measure'. This

---

[1] NOTE: All references to Mein Kampf, unless otherwise stated, will come from the following translation. After any quotation for this publication, there will simply be the two letters, MK and the page numbers. Hitler, A. (1939) *Mein Kampf*. England. Hurst and Blackett Ltd.

corrective measure would see the murder of nearly 300,000 unwitting patients whose relatives were mostly duped into delivering them into the care of the Nazi state. More than this, the T4 programme would develop the personnel, systems and methods of murder that would be transferred directly to the death camps. There, millions would die.

WHAT THIS IS CONNECTED TO

The War: doctors become murderers

When World War Two began with the invasion of Poland, Hitler seemed to see two things clearly. One was a problem and the other was an opportunity. The problem, as Hitler saw it, was what to do with those in the conquered territories who were not, as proffered in Mein Kampf, the 'best in quality'; the opportunity was the chance to put into practice his long held desire to rid the German population once and for all (as well as expediently) of those that had a 'life unworthy of living' and lived 'burdensome lives'. The 'Sterilisation Law' of 1933 was the first step towards that destination - but this was too slow a pace for Hitler, euthanasia was much faster. Euthanasia would solve the problem and take advantage of the opportunity. The war provided the distraction, the cover, and the justification to begin the wholesale (though still secret) extermination of those 'harmful' genes that might infect the pure German people within their national borders and those without. Karl Brandt, Hitler's personal physician and the man who was given co-responsibility for T4 by Hitler's letter of October 1939, gave post-war testimony at Nuremberg (1945-46). In this testimony, Brandt stated that,

> "The Führer was of the opinion that [killing the incurably ill] would be easier and smoother to carry out in wartime, since the public resistance . . . from the churches would not play such a

prominent role amidst the events of wartime as it otherwise would."[2]

Picture 2: Karl Brandt, Hitler's physician and one of the men responsible for T4, hearing judgement at the Nuremberg Trials

Let us not forget that Hitler, and a great many other Germans, blamed defeat in World War One on the genetic weaknesses of her soldiers, in part because of miscegenation (interbreeding of races, in this case between Aryan Germans and *others*), in part because those with hereditary illnesses had been 'permitted' to procreate. Compounding this problem, as Hitler saw it, was the wartime 'wastage' of genetically preferred Germans on the battlefield, leaving the weak back in Germany to multiply. In the early days of World War Two, Hitler had made the decision that whatever the future was to hold for Germany, it should not be a repeat of 1914-1918. The euthanasia programme, as

---

[2] This is quotation from Karl Brandt giving testimony after the war. The quotation is part of an exhibit in the *United States Memorial and Holocaust Museum*.

ordained by the Führer's letter of October 1939, would accelerate his desire to create genetic hygiene in Germany and, crucially, legalise it, *"...for it is never by war that nations are ruined, but by the loss of their powers of resistance, which are exclusively a characteristic of pure racial blood"*. (MK p.231)

The Final Solution

If the war provided the 'cover' and legal justification for the large scale euthanising of those Germans (and later, peoples of other nationalities) considered either to be an economic or genetic burden upon the state, then it also set a diabolical precedent. Hitler had conflated his anti-Semitism with the apparent National Socialist truism that racial cross-fertilisation had led to the genetic weakness of Aryan Germans long before the *T4* euthanasia programme began, but now that it *had* begun, the precedent was set for establishing criteria by which legal murder could take place. As history unfortunately would show us, the transition from a state-ordained euthanasia programme based upon apparent physical disorders (as unconscionable as that was) to a state-ordained euthanasia programme based upon apparent racial 'disorders', appears not to have been troubled by moral considerations. The *T4* programme set not only the precedent for the future genocide of Europe's Jews, it also generated the physical infrastructure and provided the willing personnel to carry it out. More than this, it created in the minds of those ordering and executing the Final Solution, a legal and philosophical foundation upon which their 'justifications' for the atrocities they would commit could be built.

> *"At the beginning of the War, or even during the War, if twelve or fifteen thousand of these Jews who were corrupting the nation had been forced to submit to poison-gas, just as hundreds of thousands of our best German workers from every social stratum and from every trade and calling had to face it in the field, then the millions of sacrifices made at the front would not have been in*

vain. On the contrary: If twelve thousand of these malefactors had been eliminated in proper time probably the lives of a million decent men, who would be of value to Germany in the future, might have been saved." (MK Vol II, p.518)

The *T4* programme began the systemic organisation of the euthanasia policy with the establishment in 1939 of the *Reich Committee for the Scientific Registering of Serious Hereditary and Congenital Illnesses*. A decree would be issued in the same year that required Germany's doctors and midwives to complete a section on a form whenever a child was born, detailing any observed physical or mental 'defects'. These 'defects' included anything from Down's Syndrome, and paralysis, to physical malformations and 'idiocy'. As the T4 programme grew, the criteria, as well as the process, for selection became far less rigorous. The forms would then be sent to Tiergartenstrasse 4 for review by the resident physicians, none of whom would ever set eyes upon the patients nor their medical records, over whom they wielded the power of life or death. Three medical professionals would review each case (perhaps hundreds at a time) and determine whether the life of the child should be brought to an end by marking the form with either a '+' or a '-'. A '+' meant death, while a '-' meant life. In addition, reviews were made of all Germany's medical facilities, from psychiatric wards to palliative care homes, and similar assessments were made of their patients - adult and child. Again, the assessment forms would then be processed at Tiergartenstrasse 4 in the same manner as detailed above.

Once it had been decided at Tiergartenstrasse 4 that a patient was to be marked for death, then instruction would be sent to the facility holding them that they were to be transferred to one of six 'euthanasia centres' at *Grafeneck, Brandenburg, Bernburg, Hartheim, Sonnenstein,* and *Hadamar,* all of which were existing psychiatric hospitals. The number of centres would rise significantly as the war progressed, spreading across national borders. It is important to remember that, for the most part, parents and relatives of the patients were told that their loved ones were being transferred in order to receive more specialist care. No visitor was ever allowed access to their relatives once the transfer had been completed. They would, in fact, never see them again; they would usually receive a death certificate claiming that the patient had died of some natural cause, such as pneumonia.

An entirely new bureaucracy developed in order to identify, separate, transfer, and then execute Germany's 'burdensome' peoples. Initially, the T4 programme killed the patients in its 'care' by lethal injection but this was later refined in order to kill more people more efficiently. A whole range of ad hoc murder systems evolved that would eventually settle on mass gassing as the 'best fit' solution. Gases including carbon monoxide were used to poison the unfortunate victims of the euthanasia programme - often being administered in, what appeared to be, communal showers, by men in white coats. Once the war started, it wasn't simply Germany's 'burdensome' peoples that became part of the Euthanasia programme: Polish adults with similar disabilities became the target of more direct methods of murder - SS bullets. However, ultimately, the vast majority of those victims of the expanded T4 programme would succumb to the brutal efficiency of asphyxiation by gassing.

Although the programme would eventually be uncovered by the public and disbanded in 1941 (in reality it was merely forced underground and away from Germany), the death total has been estimated by some to be as high as 400,000. In order to murder 400,000 people, a diabolical scientific method including observation, measurement, experiment, and modification would create a wide-ranging state-run administration responsible for the effective management of the protocols of death. The administration, thus created, would provide everything that was to be required - from the tools to the expertise to the implicit 'justification' - for the Final Solution. Without taking anything away from the tragedy of the hundreds of thousands forcibly euthanised by the *T4* programme, it was merely a successful dress-rehearsal for the millions to come.

WHAT YOU DIDN'T KNOW WILL BLOW YOUR MIND

How American lawmakers helped shape Hitler's views on eugenics

Across the pages of this book it should be evident that, although Nazi Germany ultimately declared war upon the United States, Hitler held many aspects of the American republic in high regard, not the least of which was the 'pioneering' work in, and whole-hearted embracing of, the pseudoscience behind selective human breeding, by many within the US.

Littered throughout *Mein Kampf* (published in 1925/26) are references lauding American racialism. In Chapter XI, titled *Race and People*, he holds up American anti-miscegenation practices as an example to be followed:

> *"But in North America the Teutonic element, which has kept its racial stock pure and did not mix it with any other racial stock, has come to dominate the American Continent and will remain master of it as long as that element does not fall a victim to the habit of adulterating blood."* (MK p223-4)

It is known that, while incarcerated in Landsberg Prison after the failed Munich Putsch (Hitler's attempt to seize power in Bavaria in 1923), Hitler spent a great deal of time absorbed in books by such people as Charles Davenport (founder of the Eugenics Record Office in New York), Leon Whitney (president of the American Eugenics Society), and Madison Grant (author of the racialist tome *The Passing of the Great Race*). According to Edwin Black, in his extraordinary book *War Against the Weak: Eugenics and America's Campaign to Create a*

Master Race, Hitler sent letters to two of these men - Whitney and Grant - thanking them for their words and inspiration and claiming that Grant's book was his 'Bible'. Judging by these letters Hitler admired the men almost as much as their ideas.

In concert with turn of the century American concerns about immigration, economic stability, and racialism (in favour of W.A.S.P.'s, naturally), eugenics became a very attractive proposition to many who happened to be of the correct ethnic background. After attempts to get bills passed through the state legislatures of Michigan and Pennsylvania, Indiana became the first state to pass laws supporting enforced sterilisation in 1907. Other states followed on the heels of Indiana. In 1927, the Supreme Court ruled in *Buck v. Bell* that forced sterilisation was (provided certain criteria were fulfilled) entirely constitutional. None other than Oliver Wendell Holmes Jr - perhaps the most influential judge in the history of US jurisprudence - wrote the decision in this case, stating,

> *"We have seen more than once that the public welfare may call upon the best citizens for their lives. It would be strange if it could not call upon those who already sap the strength of the State for these lesser sacrifices...to prevent our being swamped with incompetence. It is better for all the world, if instead of waiting to execute degenerate offspring for crime, or to let them starve for their imbecility, society can prevent those who are manifestly unfit from continuing their kind...* **Three generations of imbeciles are enough**". (Buck v. Bell, 274 U.S. 200 (1927))

Thereafter, tens of thousands of American people adjudged to be physically and intellectually disabled - including criminals - were forcibly sterilised. All without their consent. Many without even the knowledge that they had been so treated. The *Law for the Prevention of Hereditarily Diseased Offspring* ('Sterilisation Law'), passed in Nazi Germany in 1933, was almost certainly modelled on a law proposed by American eugenicist, Harry H. Laughlin, which accelerated forced sterilisation throughout the United States after 1922.

Picture 3: Indianapolis Statehouse

How German Catholics helped bring an end to Aktion T4

Unfortunately, the Catholic Church maintained a rather deafening silence on the issue of Nazi anti-Semitism and state-ordained persecution of Europe's Jews. Fortunately, the same cannot be said of its volume when it came to speaking out about the euthanising of those who were caught up in the *T4* net. The majority of the *Aktion T4* programme took place on German soil and, as such, often came into direct and public conflict with the systems of charity and care organised by Germany's Catholic Church. Although initially designed to be covert, the *T4* programme was revealed reasonably swiftly by the many relatives who brought their concerns to wider attention via the communication networks embedded within the German Catholic Church. As a result, once the existence of

T4 was confirmed, the Church was able to mobilise its media resources to put pressure on the Nazis.

Both Richard Evans and Ian Kershaw[3] are clear in their assertions that the public protests led by the Bishop of Munster, August von Galen, were the most vocal, explicit, organised, and confrontational that had been voiced during the entirety of Nazi rule. The widespread pressure, which would later come from Pope Pius XII himself, helped Hitler make the decision to conclude the *T4* programme.

Unfortunately, the programme merely went further underground, further afield, and mutated into the Final Solution - something about which the Catholic Church was conspicuously less vocal. One of the victims of the *T4* programme was one of Joseph Ratzinger's cousins. Joseph Ratzinger would go on to become Pope Benedict XVI.

Heinrich Gross and the brains of children

Austrian doctor Heinrich Gross died in December 15th, 2005, having led a rather glittering career as a psychiatrist, paediatric neurologist and court appointed expert in issues related to cases of insanity. From 1955 he was the head prison physician at the hospital complex Am Steinhof and was on the board of management of the Ludwig Boltzmann Institute. Gross was also awarded the *Medal für Wissenschaft und Kunst 1* (Medal of Honour for Science & Art) by the Austrian government in 1975. He also murdered children, authorised the murder of children and adults, and oversaw the torturous experimentation on both. Part of Am Steinhof was known as Am Spielgelgrund

---

[3] Kershaw's views on the significance of Bishop von Galen's outspoken opposition to euthanasia and other Nazi actions are contained throughout works such as, *Hitler: A Biography*. Similarly, Evans' are to be found in many of his works such as his lecture, '*Ordinary Germans and the Final Solution*'.

(named for a nearby street) - and it was here that hundreds of children were experimented upon and killed by teams led by Gross.

Picture 4: Heinrich Gross

Despite his role in the Austrian 'chapter' of the *T4* programme, he was able to escape prison or verdicts of guilty due to problems associated with the passage of time, legal jurisdiction, and his apparent dementia. However, hundreds of testimonies by patients incarcerated in Am Steinhof while he was resident, revealed repeated horrific experiences at his hands or those of his subordinates. Despite this, Gross was still able to rise, professionally, in the world of Austrian neurology and psychiatry. One of the reasons he was rated so highly was because of his 'children's brain library' - the envy of many paediatric physicians throughout the country - from which he could draw his analysis and conclusions. It was only in 1997, when a researcher published a paper detailing the provenance of the brains, that a subsequent investigation concluded that they had substantial traces of poison, proving that the children to whom these brains belonged had been murdered. Due to his advanced age, as well as jurisdictional conflicts between

Germany and Austria, Heinrich Gross spent no time in prison before his death. Nor was he convicted of any crime.

Picture 5: Aktion T4 Memorial, Tiergarten, Berlin

2

SUNSHINE NAZIS:
HOW HITLER CONTROLLED HOLLYWOOD

WHAT YOU NEED TO KNOW

Georg Gyssling was, for nearly a decade prior to World War Two, the most hated and, quite possibly, most powerful man in Hollywood. He forced the re-editing of scripts, was able to bully directors into cutting scenes that often rendered a film almost incoherent and scared the *Motion Picture Producers and Distributors Association of America* so much that they practically only released movies of which he approved. Even the heads of the biggest studios in the country - MGM, 20th Century Fox, and Paramount - were intimidated into personally pre-screening movies for Gyssling prior to release, just so they could gauge his response. More often than not, they prostrated themselves before his demands. Georg Gyssling could make or break a movie; even a studio. Georg Gyssling was a powerhouse in Hollywood. He was also a German and a Nazi.

WHY IT'S IMPORTANT THAT YOU KNOW THIS

The Nazis, particularly Hitler, understood the powerful ability of film to influence the masses. Perhaps the greatest piece of propaganda ever committed to celluloid, was Leni Riefenstahl's controversial, Triumph of the Will, a cinematic and metaphor-laden review of the 1935 Nazi Rally at Nuremberg. Understanding this power meant that the National Socialists were profoundly sensitive to, not only the nature and content of films shown in Germany, but also those developed, created, and shown in other countries. During the late 1920's - when the NSDAP (National Socialist German Worker's Party – the Nazis) were still in their formative, yet ascendant, years, the attempt to shape their image wherever they could was a priority. Of course, this was easier within the borders of Germany than without, however, once Hitler became Chancellor in 1933, it became easier because the Nazis had the full force of the German state behind their ambitions for image control. As a result, this control extended across the globe - particularly to those areas whose raison d'être was image creation. Such as Hollywood. As counterintuitive as it sounds, the Nazis were able to influence the films that came out of Hollywood almost as easily as if they were being made in Germany.

After fighting in World War One, Georg Gyssling joined the German Foreign Service and rapidly impressed those above him. He was attached to the German consulate in New York by 1927 and from there he was sent to Los Angeles "...to serve as Hitler's official representative to the Jewish-dominated motion picture industry"[4]. Germany represented the largest market for Hollywood outside of the US and Hitler, Goebbels, and Gyssling knew that pressure could, with relative ease, be brought to bear on the studios if they made films unsuited to their finely-tuned National Socialist palate. Up until 1940, the studio heads were, more often than not, willing to sacrifice the coherence of their films and, indeed, their own moral code, if it meant that their films could be seen in Germany. The bottom line was the motivating factor behind studio leviathans like Louis B. Mayer (of MGM) and Darryl F. Zanuck (of Warner Bros./20th Century Fox) in allowing Gyssling to shape their

---

[4] Ibid

final product. Carl Laemmle, the German-born, Jewish boss of Universal Pictures, reluctantly acquiesced to the Nazis - going so far as to re-cut the classic film, *All Quiet on the Western Front*, into incomprehensibility, to satisfy the demands of German nationalists who believed it portrayed their own soldiers as cowardly and weak. Josef Goebbels whipped up such a frenzy in the German media that Laemmle bowed to the pressure. Much of the pressure was manufactured by the National Socialists who, on the 6th December 1930 purchased nearly a third of the seats at the second screening of the film in Berlin's *Mozart Hall* and, led by the Nazi Gauleiter of Berlin - Josef Goebbels - proceeded to cause a riot. Days of speeches and demonstrations followed, at which Goebbels et al berated the film as Jewish and Allied propaganda. What's notable about the success of these National Socialist actions is that they caused ripples throughout Hollywood, as studios began to count the costs of losing business in Germany. What's even more notable, is that this pressure was brought to bear by a foreign political party that weren't even in power. Even William Hays, Chairman of the *Motion Picture Producers and Distributors Association* (colloquially known as the *Hays Office*), and the man who was almost single-handedly responsible for the 'moral code' all American films had to abide by, willingly collaborated with Gyssling in ensuring no anti-Nazi films were made during the 1930's.

It is well documented that Hitler was an avid film fan - often watching at least one movie a day. Josef Goebbels, ever trying to ingratiate himself into the good books of the Führer, once gifted a dozen Disney films to Hitler at Christmas because he was known to be a fan of Mickey Mouse. Despite his proclivities for animated rodents, Hitler was very clear about the types of films which were *useful* to the National Socialist agenda. These films were generally not from Disney. Hitler was interested in motifs and messages in films that reinforced certain National Socialist tropes: anti-Semitism, sacrificial leadership, military success, and triumph through struggle. A number of Hollywood films that seemed to demonstrate these tropes and were eagerly shown in Germany under the Nazis include, *The Lives of a Bengal Lancer* with Gary Cooper, *Captains Courageous* with Spencer Tracy, and *The House of Rothschild* as it conformed to their stereotypes of Jewish bankers. Portions of this latter film were even used (illegally) in the monstrous piece of Nazi anti-Semitic propaganda, *The Eternal Jew*.

Picture 6: Hitler and Goebbels overseeing a Nazi film production

The other side of this particular coin was that, while Hitler and Goebbels saw film as an instrument of propaganda, they were equally passionate about the need for censorship of those movies that didn't accord with their own ideological beliefs. It was with this in mind that Georg Gyssling was dispatched to Los Angeles - to manipulate American studios into censoring their own films. For a time, particularly in the 1930's, Hollywood bowed to the pressure of the Nazis. In many respects, National Socialists in Los Angeles and the wider state of California represented a veritable fifth column of Germans looking to reshape American mainstream media in their own image – much more of which is detailed below.

Perhaps the single most obvious 'success' that Gyssling had in exerting pressure on American film-making was that of keeping the film, *The Mad Dog of Europe*, written in 1933 by the man who would write Citizen Kane, from being made. Herman J. Manckiewicz had decided that a film needed to be made that visualised the Nazi treatment of Jews in Germany, and so set about writing a screenplay. The screenplay went to Sam Jaffe, a producer at RKO, who instantly saw the value (in all senses) of producing a film of this kind. As soon as word got out that a film, albeit in its nascent development stages, was being considered and that this would be the first film to directly tackle - and criticise - the Nazi regime, a ripple went through Hollywood. Gyssling's preventive mechanisms clicked into gear. Obstructions and objections immediately raised themselves in front of *The Mad Dog of Europe*. Despite being driven by 'super-agent' Al Rosen, who flung all his energies into getting the film made, this first real Hollywood challenge to Hitler's Germany, was dead in the water. From the Hays Office, to Louis B. Mayer, to Twentieth Century Fox, the pressure brought to bear by Gyssling, was suffocating. Each and every avenue explored by Rosen was closed off because American studios made too much money in Germany for them to risk even contemplating an American project so clearly critical of the National Socialists. The reality of American media and commerce being dictated by the financial demands of a foreign dictatorship, regardless of the moral sacrifices made by those in control of the businesses - let's not forget that a significant proportion of them were Jewish - should generate serious surprise.

WHAT THIS IS CONNECTED TO

Anti-Semitism and a judenfrei California

Gyssling was a German and a member of the NSDAP. His remit was to shape Hollywood fare, as far as the pressure he could exert would allow him to do so, into an image that did not undermine the nationalist character of Germany as ordained by Hitler. He was able to do this because the leverage he had was, for the most part, economic. The large studios (not including Warner Bros. who, courageously, withdrew from Germany in 1934) almost always bowed to the pecuniary pressure brought to bear by Gyssling and the German Film Code, which threatened to expel them from the German market. Paramount, Universal, 20th Century Fox and such, usually succumbed to the threats and adapted their films into sanitised versions, absent of any criticism directed towards Germany. Most of the studios remained in Germany until France capitulated under the power of the Nazi Wehrmacht (the unified German armed forces). Despite the heads of these prominent studios being Jewish, many refused to publicly denounce the increasing levels of oppression being visited upon the Jews of Germany until well after the point of no return had been passed, mostly in the cause of protecting their businesses interests.

Unfortunately, the history of Nazi influence over American cinema was not limited to the coerced censorship of films and scripts so that they reflected well or, at least, not badly on Germany or the National Socialists. At the same time, a darker form of manipulation was taking place and little public resistance was ever offered by the studios to it: a call by Goebbels and the *Reichsfilmkammer* to cull Jews from German and Hollywood film production in an attempt to make them Judenrein, or 'clean of Jews'. Lists of Jewish men and women were drawn up by the Reich Ministry of Public Enlightenment and Propaganda and given over to the major studios. Upon these lists were the names of people they did not want to be employed - either in Germany or Hollywood. From scriptwriters to directors, creatives within the industry were singled out for removal or 'erasure' (names were changed, film credits 'fudged'). In his excellent piece for The Hollywood Reporter, entitled *The Chilling History of How Hollywood Helped*

Hitler, Paul Rogers describes how, not only did hundreds of Jews employed in the studios owned by the big Hollywood moguls lose their livelihoods, but that,

> *"Over the next few years, the studios actively cultivated personal contacts with prominent Nazis. In 1937, Paramount chose a new manager for its German branch: Paul Thiefes, a member of the Nazi Party. The head of MGM in Germany, Frits Strengholt, divorced his Jewish wife at the request of the Propaganda Ministry. She ended up in a concentration camp."[5]*

In her piece for The Weekly Standard, *Nazis in Tinseltown*, Leslie Epstein explains how, in private, the moguls would quietly support anti-Nazi groups such as the Hollywood Anti-Nazi League, and that none of them "...save the suspect Walt Disney, wished the new Germany well", but ultimately their actions were "...largely barren"[6]. Even when the war was being waged and America had pitted itself against the Nazis, the thread of anti-Semitism and weak resistance continued. According to Epstein, the only Hollywood film made during the entirety of the war to even mention the word 'Jew' or 'Jewish', was *Mr. Skeffington*, a film written and produced in 1944 by both her father and uncle - Philip and Julius Epstein.

It must be noted at this point that none of the studio heads could be said to have collaborated with the Nazis, in the sense that they ever either actively supported Hitler, the National Socialists, or the Third Reich - to assert such would be absurd. What they did do was adapt to the economic pressures exerted by the Nazi German state and the politico-moral pressures exerted by the Hays Office. In addition, a not entirely

---

[5] Rogers, P. (2013). *The Chilling History of How Hollywood Helped Hitler.* Available at: *https://www.hollywoodreporter.com/news/how-hollywood-helped-hitler-595684. Accessed August 2018.*
[6] Epstein, L. (2018). *Nazis in Tinseltown.* Available at: https://www.weeklystandard.com/leslie-epstein/nazis-in-tinseltown (Accessed: November 2018)

convincing argument was proffered by many within and without the Jewish-American community (including many in positions of power and influence) that any overt criticism levelled at the Nazis would only serve to worsen the treatment of Jews in Germany. Perhaps more could and should have been done to resist these forces of National Socialism by those that were able, relatively easily it must be said, to frame Hollywood movie production within their own ideological parameters. Perhaps, also, to lay too much blame at the feet of American businessmen who, patently, had no notion of how Hitler's regime would ultimately attempt to destroy Europe's Jews, is unhelpful. This does not, however, negate the outcome: American studio film production was, both directly and indirectly, almost entirely neutralised by the likes of Gyssling. Unfortunately, the influence of National Socialism in America as a whole, and California in particular, was not limited to the narrow reach of officials in the employ of the Nazi state, such as Georg Gyssling. A much more homegrown fascism, white nationalism, and anti-Semitism was taking root in American public discourse.

Der Tag (The Day of Victory): American Nazis

In the twilight of the 1920's and the dawn of the 1930's, Americans were focussed on a number of pressing (and painfully distracting) issues, none of which was the growing power of Hitler and the National Socialists, 4000 miles away. Why would Americans be concerned with problems in Germany, when they had so many of their own to concern themselves with: The Red Scare, the growth of organised crime, the whereabouts of the Lindbergh baby, the social and economic problems associated with Prohibition, problems associated with the repeal of Prohibition and, lest we forget, the Wall Street Crash and the Great Depression. There was very little energy leftover for the average American to worry about the leadership of a distant country, when their own country seemed to be overwhelmed by the extreme vacillations of twentieth century life. It was, perhaps, as much of America was focussed on matters close to home, that two things happened almost unnoticed: 1) National Socialism crept into the near-mainstream of American political society; 2) Hitler's emissaries in Los Angeles, and the Ministry of Propaganda back in Germany, began to shape the cinema of Hollywood.

The significance of these two narratives should not be underestimated. In his phenomenal book, *Hitler in Los Angeles: How Jews Foiled Nazi Plots Against Hollywood and America*, Steven J. Ross details the rise in influence of both of these narratives (as well as many others), from the first public and open meeting of Nazis in Los Angeles just a handful of months after Hitler became Chancellor of Germany, to the profound impact of "…the most reviled Nazi in Los Angeles"[7] - Georg Gyssling - on Hollywood. Unfortunately, Gyssling was not the only Nazi in America.

In the year 1890, William Dudley Pelley was born into an impoverished Methodist family who lived in Lynn Massachusetts. Pelley is something of an American success story - through diligence and a voracious appetite for the written word he began publishing his own work by the age of 19. Making himself into a successful journalist, he spent time abroad covering the Russian Civil War, and then returned to America to have two of his short stories win the prestigious O. Henry Award for outstanding writing. Moving to California, Pelley began screenwriting and had two of his works made into major films. In 1929, an essay he published in America Magazine, entitled Seven Minutes in Eternity, became a nationwide phenomenon. In 1931 he created his own

---

[7] Ross, Steven J. (2017) *The Hollywood Nazi who Spied for America*. Available at: https://www.washingtonpost.com/news/made-by-history/wp/2017/10/25/the-hollywood-nazi-who-spied-for-america/?noredirect=on&utm_term=.a490fc6384ed (Accessed: September 2018)

publishing company, Galahad Press, and opened a college in Asheville, North Carolina. In 1936, William Dudley Pelley even ran for president. From poverty to a presidential election in 46 years is quite an achievement. He also founded the *Silver Legion* - an American fascist, anti-Semitic, white nationalist paramilitary group modelled after Hitler's Brownshirts, the SA.

Picture 7: William Dudley Pelley – creator of the Silver Legion

The Silver Legion, whose members were known as the Silver Shirts, and wore a silver shirt emblazoned with a large scarlet 'L', a blue tie, a hat, blue trousers, and often carried pistols, became the largest pro-Nazi organization in the United States. Its headquarters were to be at, what would become known as, Murphy Ranch, a 55-acre plot purchased from Hollywood legend, Will Rogers, in north Los Angeles. You can visit this now-graffitied, burned out edifice on a number of morbid historical Hollywood tours. Nestled in Rustic Canyon in an affluent area of Pacific Palisades, Murphy Ranch was repurposed and remodelled to accommodate long periods of isolation - a huge water tank, fuel tank and generator rooms were to sustain Pelley and his Silver Legion during a white, fascist, nationalist-Christian re-taking of America, which was supposed to begin from this location. According to a number of historians and journalists (Randy Young, Betty Lou and others), this compound was being constructed using funds being indirectly channelled from Germany through a Nazi agent in the US known as Herr Schmidt. Some, most likely spurious, accounts have Murphy ranch as being constructed specifically for the arrival of the Führer, once America had been overrun by its homegrown National Socialists. Startlingly, this was not the most terrifying development in California during this time.

Nazi Flags on Main Street: The German American Bund & murderous plots in California

The Amerikadeutscher Volksbund, or the German American Bund, was an organisation established in the United States by both German expatriates and German-Americans looking to accomplish a number of objectives: maintain a certain attachment within the community to traditional German cultural values, to help assimilate newly arrived German émigrés into American society, and to ensure involvement in American political life, so as to help promote the aspirations of the diaspora. The Bund was created in 1936 out of the ashes of its forerunner, the Friends of New Germany. *Friends* was dissolved because of near constant congressional scrutiny from the Special Committee on Un-American Activities Authorized to Investigate Nazi Propaganda and Certain Other Propaganda Activities. It was administered (vaguely in keeping with Nazi Party organisation) through three gaue (regional districts): West, East, and Mid America. Growing into a substantial organisation that stretched across the United States, its nearly 70 regional divisions and numerous youth camps, promoted both Germanism and Americanism. Alongside this dual patriotism, the Bund also tended to reflect the ideological bent of its originary nation. What this means is that, from its inception in 1936, the German American Bund was a National Socialist German-American organisation.

Picture 8: Insignia/flag of the German American Bund

In the cauldron of dissatisfaction felt by many Americans who had spent too many years living with the effects of the Great Depression and who hated President Franklin D. Roosevelt's New Deal (which was often refashioned by those inclined to the right of the political spectrum, as the 'Jew Deal'), anti-democratic, nationalist forces promising solutions, began to mix openly with an anti-Semitism that offered a convenient scapegoat for their dissatisfaction. Into this broiling crucible was poured the resources and agenda of the German American Bund, who deliberately looked to carry the message of Hitler's Germany directly to those that would listen. And, unfortunately, there were many who wanted to - particularly in California.

Picture 9: German American Bund march in New York, 30th October 1939

By the time World War Two was in its fourth year, the leader of the German American Bund - Fritz Kuhn - had spent a great portion of it in prison. The House Un-American Activities Committee and its Chairman, Congressman Martin Dies, had expended great energies in the lead up to the war investigating the activities of the German American Bund as part of its remit to challenge any organisation sympathetic to the Nazis. It was, however, New York City's District Attorney, Thomas E. Dewey, who filed an indictment against Kuhn and had him convicted for embezzlement. While in prison Kuhn had his American citizenship revoked and almost immediately following his release in June 1943, he was re-arrested as an 'enemy agent' and interned until the end of the war, whereupon he was deported to Germany. The significance of the war time travails of Fritz Kuhn should go some way in forcing home just how influential he and the Bund had become in America - so much so that the federal and local New York government wanted him arrested and its activities suspended. Unfortunately, for many in America - particularly those in southern California - this suspension was a little long in coming.

Picture 10: Leader of the German American Bund, Fritz Kuhn

On February 20th, 1939, the German American Bund held a rally in Madison Square Garden. The rear of the stage was draped in forty feet high flags - both of the United States (in an unusual rendering) and of the Bund. The Bund's two enormous flags each comprised of a shield and a powerful gold swastika. At the centre of the array of flags hung another imposing forty-foot image - that of George Washington. It would be hard to imagine another night in the history of Madison Square Garden at which such an incongruous set of imagery ornamented the walls. While there was pageantry on the east coast of America, there was an altogether more sinister role being played out by the German American Bund on the west coast.

In his book, *Hitler in Los Angeles: How the Jews Foiled Nazi Plots against Hollywood and America*, Professor Steven J. Ross demonstrates how the Nazi state had quickly decided that their point of entry into the US, in terms of their propaganda, financial assistance, and agitation, would not be New York -

which the Nazis called "Jew York"[8] - but Los Angeles. According to Ross, in Los Angeles there was

> "...a long history of anti-Semitism, racism, Ku Klux Klan activities and right-wing demagogues. And the port was never monitored. And so the Nazis were able to send their ships to L.A., and on every ship there was always a Gestapo officer. When they would dock in L.A., the head of the [German-American group] Bund here would go down to the docks and receive money, propaganda and secret orders from Germany."[9]

Although the big studios in Hollywood were run, in the main, by Jewish moguls and the creative population of the cinema industry was dominated by Jews, those who made up the rank and file of both the industry and its ancillary businesses, from the drivers to the security guards, were not. In fact, a vein of anti-Semitism coursed through the body of the west coast entertainment centre of the world. The blood type carried by this vein was not unique to show business - it filled the arteries of many who lived and worked across southern California.

There is a park in southern California, just north of Los Angeles, called Crescenta Valley Community Regional Park. In 2017 a sign was erected in this park that attempted to pay homage to the previous name of a portion of the park. The sign caused a furore among some within the local community and the mounting pressure ultimately resulted in its removal. The sign that caused so much consternation strove, with goodwill and sincerity, to recollect the original German-American contribution to the area. The top of the sign read 'Willkommen zum". Underneath, and scripted beautifully across its full width, the words "Hindenburg Park" projected outwards. In the

---

[8] Morrison, P. (2017). *How Hitler's fascism almost took hold in Los Angeles.* Available at: https://www.latimes.com/opinion/op-ed/la-ol-patt-morrison-steven-ross-nazi-los-angeles-20170927-htmlstory.html. (Accessed: September 2018)
[9] Ibid

1930's Hindenburg Park was host to several Bund rallies, political gatherings and family picnics for its members. When the Bund convened its members at Hindenburg Park, whether it was for social purposes or political (they often converged), Swastikas in flag, sculpture, picture and even cake form, would boldly decorate the event. Counterintuitively, the flying of the swastika was not an uncommon sight during the 1930's in Southern California. On the cover of Professor Ross' book, *Hitler in Los Angeles...*, there is a photograph of Broadway, arguably one of the main streets in pre- World War Two Los Angeles (in fact, the street was viewed by many at the time as the centre of the city), lined with fluttering Nazi Swastika flags. The German American Bund were not the only organisation in California looking to stimulate pro-Nazi sentiment, but it was the most influential - and potentially the most dangerous.

A rampant homegrown hatred of communism and a conflation of it with Judaism, led to a marked uptick in, what was already a prevalent, anti-Semitism in the US. In many parts of America, being a Nazi was preferable to being a communist. With the right amount of stimulation by those associated with the German American Bund, it didn't take long for serious dangers to both California's Jewish population, and the business interests of the state, to emerge. Once again, Professor Ross offers the evidence of staggering plots to destabilize factories by local agents of the Nazis who would blow up machinery. Other plots looked to massacre vast numbers of people in Jewish-populated neighbourhoods, mass hang Jews and prominent politicians, murder movie stars such as Charlie Chaplin, and use poisonous gas to fumigate large community buildings housing American Jews. The men who plotted these deeds were Americans. Some were Nazis, some 'merely' hated communists. Others wanted to rid America of Jews. Others wanted to start a nationwide revolution with an open invite to Adolf Hitler.

One of the central defenders against this Nazi activity in Los Angeles, and a man (along with his courageous recruits) who, according to both Ross and Leslie Epstein, probably did more to protect the Jewish communities of California than anyone else - whether in government or out of it - was Leon Lewis. Epstein, in her article describes the extraordinary resistance of certain individuals and groups in California who went to great efforts, and at great costs, risking great penalties to undermine the efforts of Nazi elements within one of America's most populous states[10]. Leon Lewis, was one of these individuals, as was Joseph Roos; the Los Angeles Jewish Community Committee (LAJCC) was one such group. Lewis, in particular, did more than most within California - particularly those who had the means and the reason to do more - to combat the organised anti-Semitism of the Silver Shirts, the German American Bund, and the Nazi state itself. The defining characteristic (as well as absolute and non-negotiable element) of National Socialist dogma - anti-Semitism - was exported to Los Angeles in a manner so brazen and explicit that it almost beggars belief. Almost. As you have already read, this racialist dogma was not merely accepted by many Americans on the west coast as an unpleasant side effect of external economic pressures (the Great Depression), it was positively welcomed in some quarters and actively encouraged in others.

Horrified by the open anti-Semitism and promotion of National Socialist ideals in California, Leon Lewis, a private citizen and war veteran, took it upon himself to recruit 'spies' (most of whom were not Jews) to infiltrate the various Nazi groups and collect evidence to present to the authorities. Although initially resistant to his data, the authorities began to investigate and, ultimately, his efforts - as well those of his colleagues (for whom he raised funds in order to pay) - reaped

---

[10] Epstein, L. (2018). *Nazis in Tinseltown*. Available at:
https://www.weeklystandard.com/leslie-epstein/nazis-in-tinseltown
(Accessed: November 2018)

rewards as the state and federal governments began to take seriously the threats being posed to American citizens, as well as the American way of life. For a thorough examination of Lewis and his profoundly courageous efforts against the very real threats already described, do take the time to read the works cited above.

WHAT YOU DIDN'T KNOW WILL BLOW YOUR MIND

All Quiet on the...world front

It wasn't simply that Hollywood had to bow to the editing demands on their films that would show in Germany. Despite making the requested edits to *All Quiet on the Western Front*, after the furore orchestrated by Goebbels against the film in Germany, President of Universal Pictures, Carl Laemmle, had to ensure that those edits were replicated throughout the world. In short, everywhere the film was to be shown, it had to conform to German Foreign Office demands. When it was discovered that an unedited print of the film was being shown in two markets - El Salvador and Spain - Universal had to make a public apology and remove all such prints from circulation.

Carl Laemmle, President of Universal Pictures and saviour of hundreds of German Jews

Karl Lämmle left the small German village of Laupheim in Germany at the age of 17. Booked on the SS Neckar from Germany when he was 17 years old, the young Karl voyaged to the US in 1884 and almost immediately began building a life for himself. Born into a Jewish Family in the Kingdom of Württemberg in southern Germany and, following in the footsteps of his older brother, he moved to America leaving his close relatives and friends behind. Laemmle eventually settled in Chicago, married and had a son. By all accounts, the newly naturalized German immigrant was an ebullient, wide-smiling lover of life. He also had a keen eye for an opportunity. Having noticed the early enthusiasm for shop-front nickelodeons (small converted shops in which movies would be projected – all for a nickel) he used his savings to open his own, called *White Front*[11].

Picture 11: President of Universal Pictures, Carl Laemmle

The success of his early forays into film presentation enabled a move to New York, where he set up *Independent Motion Pictures* (IMP), but not before successfully challenging Thomas Edison (no less) in court over his attempts to monopolise motion pictures. IMP would, through mergers and acquisitions, ultimately become *Universal Pictures* with Carl Laemmle as its President.

---

[11] Mansky, J. (2017) *This Hollywood Titan Foresaw the Horrors of Nazi Germany. Available at:* https://www.smithsonianmag.com/arts-culture/this-hollywood-titan-foresaw-horrors-nazi-germany-180961828/ (Accessed November 2018)

Picture 12. Laemmle's first real film production company

Universal was the studio behind the film *All Quiet on the Western Front*, which was banned in Germany as a result of National Socialist opposition. Under significant pressure from the German state, the studio had to cull core elements of the film deemed unacceptable to the German Film Code, for it to be shown *anywhere* in the world. What must not be forgotten, however, is that the President of Universal Pictures exerted immeasurable energies trying to get the film shown without cuts, going so far as to successfully persuade perhaps the most powerful man in world media at the time - William Randolph Hearst[12] - to petition the German government to allow the film to be seen unedited. Such was the outcry created - mostly by the NSDAP - that, even with such heavyweight backing, the studio was forced into cutting significant scenes from the film. There wasn't a great deal Carl Laemmle could do to stop the film being neutered by the German government. Ultimately, the film was banned in its entirety after Hitler came to power in 1933.

---

[12] American publishing and business magnate – the person upon whom the character Citizen Kane was based. Profoundly wealthy and influential.

Picture 13: Laemmle's 1930 film, banned by the Nazis.

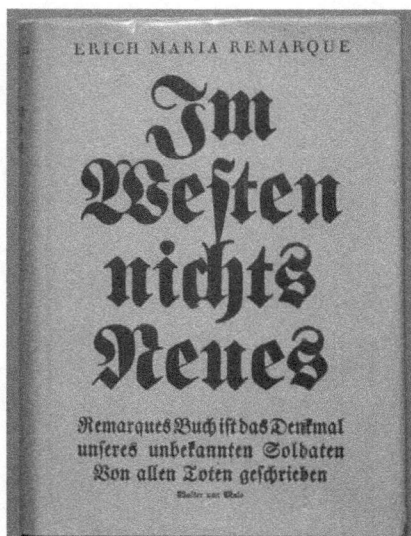

Picture 14: In Germany, the film/book was called Im Westen nichts Neues (In the West Nothing New)

The impotence he felt in regard to his inability to have *All Quiet on the Western Front* shown in its complete form was clearly something that remained with him throughout the rest of his life, because he spent much of his time thereafter trying to remove German Jews from the vicious grip of the Nazis. Even going so far as to resign, in April 1936, from the company he founded, to better concentrate his efforts and resources to this cause. On the 150th anniversary of Carl Laemmle's birthday, Dr Rainer Schimpf curated an exhibition at the Haus der Geschichte Baden-Württemberg in Stuttgart, Germany. The exhibition ran from 9th December 2016 - 30th July 2017 and it detailed two entwined elements of Laemmle's life: his contributions to the film industry and his contributions to protecting the lives of Germany's Jews from the violence of National Socialism. Even before the Nazis came to power, the President of Universal Pictures was keenly concerned for Europe's Jews, should the Hitler's Party take control in Germany. In a letter of January 28th, 1932, Laemmle wrote to William Randolph Hearst that,

> *"I am almost certain that Hitler's rise to power, because of his obvious militant attitude toward the Jews, would be the signal for a general physical onslaught on many thousands of defenseless Jewish men, women and children in Germany, and possibly in Central Europe as well, unless something is done soon to definitely establish Hitler's personal responsibility in the eyes of the outside world".[13]*

The exhibition, along with a number of recent works, have sought to draw attention to Carl Laemmle's efforts in assisting the emigration of hundreds of German Jews to the United States and out of the clutches of Hitler's increasingly brutal regime. Because of particularly stringent immigration laws (the United States was still operating a quota system which limited the numbers of people that it would accept from specific

[13] Ibid

countries), the process was fraught with bureaucratic challenges. In addition, most migrants were required to have a supporting affidavit from an American sponsor who would both vouch for their character and promise to support them financially. Laemmle wrote hundreds of affidavits in support of German Jews - many of them complete strangers - who, because of his support, were successful in their immigration applications. Because of his elevated position within American business, Laemmle was also able to communicate with people capable of exerting significant influence over the situation. The exhibition contains a letter he sent to then Secretary of State, Cordell Hull exhorting him to pressure the American Consulate in Stuttgart to expedite the immigration applications. The exhibition also contains Hull's response, which is largely positive. In addition, Laemmle wrote an impassioned letter to President Franklin D. Roosevelt requesting that he intervene on behalf of a ship carrying nearly a thousand German Jews which had been refused port entry in Cuba. The *MS St. Louis*, a German liner, was essentially a refugee ship in search of sanctuary away from Germany. Ultimately, Laemmle's entreaties to Roosevelt went unheeded and the ship eventually returned to Europe, whereupon its passengers dispersed across a number of accommodating countries. It is estimated that over a quarter of those passengers who Carl Laemmle was looking to have accepted into America, were murdered in the death camps of Europe. In the movie world, Carl Laemmle's legacy is well documented and rightly lauded; in the history of those who found themselves comfortably out of the reach of the Nazis yet took on National Socialism wherever they found it, Laemmle's legacy is only beginning to receive the attention and praise it deserves.

Picture 15: The MS St. Louis leaves Hamburg for Cuba carrying over 900 German Jews. This ship and its passengers were refused entry by Havana and Washington. Ultimately, a great many were murdered by the Nazis upon their return to Europe.

Picture 16: Carl Laemmle with son Carl Jr and daughter Rosabelle

Joseph I. Breen and the Production Code Administration (PCA): protecting Nazi Germany until January 1940

Established in 1934 as a department within the *Motion Picture Producers and Distributors Association* of America, and headed by rabid anti-Semite Joseph Breen, the *Production Code Administration* was created to enforce the *Motion Picture Production Code*. This code was a set of moral protocols which studios had to follow in order for a film to receive a PCA stamp of approval. Failure to adhere rigidly to the PCA's stipulations would result in a significant financial penalty and risk a film being taken from cinemas. In his book, *Hollywood Censor: Joseph I. Breen and the Production Code of America*, Thomas Doherty claims that "...this bureaucratic functionary was one of the most powerful men in Hollywood"[14]. In order to reinforce this point, Thomas recites *Liberty Magazine's* 1936 onstage introduction to Breen as a man who has "...more influence in standardizing world thinking than Mussolini, Hitler and Stalin"[15]. Under the authority of Joseph Breen, a staunch Roman Catholic, the PCA made it a point of principle that the studios, who Breen viewed with something akin to contempt because of their Jewish controlling interests, be brought in line with his rigid view of morality and decency. Though the PCA was supposed to encourage Hollywood to self-regulate, Breen was, in reality, a nearly pathologically-driven censor. Few movies ever got past him without cuts in script or celluloid being demanded. In one area in particular, Joseph I. Breen was particularly ferocious: that of ensuring, as far as he was able to, no film disparaged Nazi Germany in any way.

In *Hollywood and Anti-Semitism: A Cultural History up to World War Two*, Steven Alan Carr quotes Breen in a letter in which he argues that Hollywood is "...95% ...Eastern Jews, the scum of

---

[14] Doherty, T. (2009) *Hollywood Censor: Joseph I. Breen and the Production Code of America*. USA: Columbia University Press. P.7.
[15] Ibid, p.8

the scum of the earth…" and that the heads of the studios were. "…simply a rotten bunch of vile people with no respect for anything beyond the making of money". He would go even further in his 'certainty' that, Will Hays may have been duped into trusting "…these lousy Jews out here [to] abide by the Code's provisions but if he did then he should be censured for his lack of proper knowledge of the breed"[16]. Of course, just because Breen was an anti-Semite, does not make him a Nazi, however, Breen was part of a vein of intolerance that coursed its way through the first sixty years of twentieth century America which often conflated being a Jew with being a communist. As a staunch anti-communist as well as a staunch anti-Semite, Breen's worldview was positioned such that he saw Hollywood as a machine for Jewish-communist propaganda that deliberately looked to paint an untruthful and provocative picture of a sovereign German state. To many, the Hollywood Anti-Nazi League was proof of this conspiracy. This fed into the powerful isolationist narrative of the time that claimed devious elements within American political and economic life were looking to convince the government to go to war in Europe for the second time in thirty years. To the eyes of many in the US, including those of Joseph Breen, Hollywood was the centre of Jewish, anti-German, anti-American, and interventionist propaganda and, as such, must be restricted.

One argument that was made by the PCA, when ordering censure of films and scripts submitted to it that were critical of Germany or National Socialism, was that, should they be allowed into production without such censure they would incite further outbursts against Germany's Jews by the Nazi state. Although this may have been true, the argument as made by Breen was largely disingenuous. His concern was always the

---

[16] Carr, Steven Alan. (2001) *Hollywood and Anti-Semitism: A Cultural History up to World War Two.* UK: Cambridge University Press. P.199

protection of the American film industry abroad, which was threatened by such flagrant 'Jewish propaganda', and the controlling of the 'moral temperature' of the most potent arm of American media. Both of these concerns were indelibly infused with a complex mix of anti-Semitism, patriotism, isolationism, anti-communism, and catholic zeal. The code specifically mandated that all nations be treated respectfully by Hollywood, with no caveat for nations acting belligerently. In *Appendix 1* of the *Motion Picture Production Code* of March 1930, under the subheading *National feelings*, it is stated that *"The history, institutions, prominent people and citizenry of other nations shall be represented fairly"*. There are any number of films and scripts handed over to Breen that he refused to endorse until they were amended because they were deemed 'pro-Jewish propaganda' or 'anti-Nazi propaganda', from Alfred Hitchcock's *Foreign Correspondent* to *Black Legion* to *Three Comrades*. Of course, there is an argument to be made that Breen and his views were merely a product of the time and not particularly out of the ordinary in American life. In a sense, and as already discussed, this is not completely untrue. However, Professor Steven J. Ross has little patience with such an argument; let us not forget that, long after the Nuremberg Laws were passed by the Nazis, which dispossessed and disenfranchised Germany's Jews and the state-organised violence of Kristallnacht decimated German-Jewish society, Joseph I. Breen and the Production Code of America were still more concerned about upsetting the Nazis than supporting any American film that drew attention to these horrors.

Confessions of a Nazi Spy: The Warner Brothers resist

Perhaps the most potent attack on German fascism (because it was really the first overt one) by the studio system of Hollywood came from the only studio that dared to challenge Georg Gyssling, the German Foreign Office, the Hays Office, the PCA (with its anti-Semitic head, Joseph Breen), and every other studio head (most of which were Jewish). That studio was Warner Bros. Through sheer force of will, Jack and Harry Warner forced into production, *Confessions of a Nazi Spy*, which was released on 6th May 1939. Such was the fear of reprisals by pro-Germany and fascist groups in Los Angeles, that on opening night the film arrived in an armoured vehicle, flanked by police officers. The studio had paid for plainclothes policemen - numbering in their hundreds - to mix, incognito, with the audience. If some accounts are to be believed, there were even men on the roof of Warner Bros. Cinema with machine guns. It would do well at this point to remember that this was an American film, produced and shown in the United States in 1939, and yet pro-Nazi groups threatened its very existence. (For a full account of the significance of this film, please see *Warner's War: Confessions of a Nazi Spy: Warner Bros., Anti-Fascism and the Politicization of Hollywood,* by Professor Steven J. Ross.)[17]

One Final Surprise: Georg Gyssling hated Hitler

Believe it or not, after everything you have just read, the man who was Hitler's Consul in Los Angeles, hated Hitler. The man who joined the Nazi Party in 1931 and was given the specific remit of suppressing anti-German and anti-Nazi films being made in Hollywood, thought the Party to be risible. Perhaps with the exception Josef Goebbels, Georg Gyssling was the man most directly responsible for promoting pro-German cinema in the US and around the world, and restricting its opposite, hated both the Party and its leader. Just let that sink in.

---

[17] Ross, Steven J. (2004) *Confessions of a Nazi Spy: Warner Bros., Anti-Fascism and the Politicisation of Hollywood.* Available at: https://searchworks.stanford.edu/view/7931846 (Accessed July 2018)

Professor of History at USC (and something of an academic legend in the history of American cinema) Steven J. Ross, is clear that Gyssling - the German who bullied movie producers into submission throughout the 1930's - led a dual life. An article he wrote in the Washington Post, *The Hollywood Nazi who spied for America*, is remarkable for its inverting of Gyssling's legacy. Without ever disputing Gyssling's hyper-censorious impact on Hollywood, Ross reveals how he was, in fact, a double agent working against Hitler. In the article, Professor Ross explains that Gyssling, "...like many in the Foreign Office, hated Hitler and felt trapped by leaders he loathed"[18]. A German nationalist (rather than a Nazi, per se), Gyssling privately decried the mess Hitler was making of his country and, counter to the public interpretation of him in Hollywood, he was not an anti-Semite. According to Ross, he "...refused to openly attack Jews or make anti-Semitic pronouncements to the press". Gyssling's own daughter defended her father as a man who encouraged a tolerant household (although one might expect her to say as much). Even if one discounts his daughter's defence, perhaps a better barometer of her father's lack of commitment to the National Socialist cause, is the fact that local Nazis (local to California and America) "...branded him a traitor"[19]. According to Ross, even Gyssling's own doctor contacted Berlin to recommend he be replaced with a more ardent National Socialist. Upon his return to Germany in 1941, he was repeatedly interrogated by the Gestapo who had their suspicions that he was not all he claimed to be.

Even more than this, Georg Gyssling was passing, indirectly, German secrets to General George C. Marshall - the Head of Army Intelligence. For years, Gyssling was revealing detailed

---

[18] Ross, Steven J. (2017) *The Hollywood Nazi who spied for America*. Available at: https://www.washingtonpost.com/news/made-by-history/wp/2017/10/25/the-hollywood-nazi-who-spied-for-america/?noredirect=on&utm_term=.907d1d7ccdd0 (Accessed November 2018)
[19] Ibid

information of the state of the German economy, the operation of Nazi 'fifth columnists' working to disrupt war munition manufacturing along the US west coast, as well as of Hitler's war plans. As the war was entering its sixth year, Ross claims that Gyssling was part of Operation Sunrise, which worked directly with the head of the Office of Strategic Services, Alan Dulles, on negotiations for German surrender in northern Italy. On top of all of this, Georg Gyssling had developed a clandestine way of assisting emigre German Jews struggling in America: a call for 'Dr Ginsberg' at his offices, was code for a German Jew in need of help inside the borders of the United States. It would seem that, to Hitler's attack dog in Hollywood, it was his duty to protect and to assist every German national, regardless of race or religion. Drawing his article in the Washington Post to a close, Ross drives home his argument - that Gyssling was not, a blinded diehard Nazi anti-Semite - by pointing out he was cleared by the American Denazification Board after the war because he could easily demonstrate "resistance rendered".

3

PERFIDIOUS ALBION:
THE COUNTRY HITLER LOVED TO HATE

WHAT YOU NEED TO KNOW

I f nothing else, Hitler was a man of very definite opinions. Even if those opinions changed frequently, which they did. One such 'definite' opinion was his view of England. It is well documented that Hitler had a respect (sometimes a grudging one) for certain elements within English (and it was English, rather than British) society and their historic accomplishments - usually military and, pointlessly, genealogically. What is also well documented, is that this opinion often mutated depending upon his personal experiences (e.g. when fighting mainly against Britain in World War One), the crowd he was addressing, the international environment Germany found itself in at the time he was speaking, and the goals he was trying to achieve. As with most authoritarian regimes, fast-held, absolute and vociferously propagandised state beliefs in foreign affairs last only as long as they serve their immediate political, diplomatic, and military ends. Hence, it is possible to trace the outlines of Hitler's worldview at any given time by examining, through his rhetoric, the wildly fluctuating attitude that Hitler held towards a country that, at different times, he both revered and detested, and with which he simultaneously wished to ally when convenient and destroy when not.

Perfidious Albion is a pejorative term that has been used throughout history, usually by England's enemies (particularly the French), but occasionally by her erstwhile allies (particularly the French), to describe an apparent tendency of England (*Albion*) to renege on her agreements or to demonstrate diplomatic duplicity (*Perifidity*). After 1938, Nazi propaganda directed at France would often use the term in attempts to drive a wedge between her and Britain - by trying to remind France of the historical 'duplicity' of England.

WHY IT'S IMPORTANT THAT YOU KNOW THIS

In her rather excellent Master of Arts thesis entitled, *The Evolution of Adolf Hitler's Weltanschauung: A Critical Study of His Rhetoric*, Carolyn Read challenged the view that Hitler maintained a largely consistent 'Weltanschauung', or World View. In her own words, Read stated that, "The Nazi leader's ideology developed according to his own personal experiences as well as the political, economic, and social climate of the era"[20]. In many ways, Hitler's view of England is very much in keeping with this claim, inasmuch as it contradicted itself on numerous occasions, but usually because of the criteria identified by Read.

This is significant because, in a very real sense, his attitude towards England can be seen as a microcosm of his broader ideological shifts. Perhaps it is too great a leap to suggest that it might be possible to determine the character of his thoughts (and hence his words and actions) at any given moment depending upon his view of England, but books have been written on less solid propositions. Regardless, for our purposes, his view of England and its leadership at specific times, is important because it helps us understand more about Hitler's

---

[20] Read, C. (1997) The Evolution of Adolf Hitler's Weltanschauung: A Critical Study of His Rhetoric. P.47. Massey University.

racialism; it helps us understand the vacillating shifts of view that peppered his time both in and out of office; it also gives us insight into his foreign impulses. Not to mention, as a simple character study, it is curious in the extreme. It would appear that Hitler's moveable view of England supports the wider interpretation held by Read, that his views were not fixed, but in a constant state of evolution. This, in itself, is significant and worth noting.

WHAT THIS IS CONNECTED TO

The Treaty of Versailles

Perhaps the early and negative incarnation of Hitler's attitude towards England is unsurprising, tempered, as it was, by two functioning narratives at the time: war and the residual Bismarckian view of German foreign policy, both of which saw England as an imperial rival and battlefield foe.

Picture 17: German Propaganda Pamphlet from 1915. Source unknown.

Once World War One was drawn to a conclusion and Germany designated as its main loser by the Treaty of Versailles, England, in the mind of Hitler and many other Germans, became conflated with a potent narrative: that the Versailles settlement was an evil concoction designed to humiliate and cripple Germany. In the German consciousness, Britain was not only coupled to the 'sadistic' terms of the Treaty, but she also began to 'enjoy' some of the well documented historical hatred that Germany had for France. In this sense, it is understandable that Hitler's early view of England, in terms of foreign policy, was profoundly negative, as demonstrated by his own words in a speech given in Munich on the 18th September 1922:

> *"We must demand a great enlightenment on the subject of the peace treaty. With thoughts of love? No! But in holy hatred against those who have ruined us."*[21]

Reflecting later in Mein Kampf, Hitler judged England's motivation for a punitive peace settlement thus:

> *"With the colonial, economical and commercial destruction of Germany, England's war aims were attained."* (MK, Vol II, P.470)

The French Invasion of the Ruhr Valley: Britain breaks with France

The French invasion of Germany's Ruhr Valley in 1923 is a staple of exam boards across the world and common knowledge to most students and teachers of European history. What is less well known - and perhaps even less thought about - is the British response to this most significant of interwar developments. The reason this is important to us, is that the

---

[21] Speech to be found at http://www.hitler.org/speeches/09-18-22.html

British response to the French invasion goes a long way in helping us understand how and why Hitler's view of 'Perfidious Albion' began to dissipate and the tide of dislike start to recede. When the Germans were unable to pay their scheduled reparations payment of "...timber and telegraph poles"[22] France chose to extract payment by invading the industrial heartland of Germany. How Britain responded to this action was, according to D. G. Williamson, in keeping with, "The often acrimonious Anglo-French debate over the interpretation of the Treaty of Versailles and the role of Germany in post-war Europe..."[23]. In short, Britain was unhappy with French actions because they destabilised Europe and restricted Germany's economic ability to help revive, "...European and indeed world economies..."[24] Even before the French occupied the Ruhr, certain British politicians and the most notable economic theorist of the time (or, perhaps, of any time), John Maynard Keynes, were arguing that the success of the British economy depended heavily upon a revision of the Treaty of Versailles and a rapprochement with Germany. It is no coincidence that, right about this time, Hitler begins to talk about England in more favourable terms. It is right about here in history that Hitler unshackles his view of England from that of France.

Hitler begins to revisit his earlier view of England as being invested, alongside France, in the destruction of Germany, actually going to so far as to *justify* English actions during the Versailles conference as being more concerned with the checking of *French* power in Europe than Germany's:

> *"To prevent the power of France from becoming too great, the only form which English negotiations could take was that of*

---

[22] Williamson, D. G. (1977) *Great Britain and the Ruhr Crisis, 1923-1924*. British Journal of International Studies, vol. 3, no. 1, pp. 70–91. *JSTOR*. Available at: www.jstor.org/stable/20096790 (Accessed: July 2018)
[23] Ibid
[24] Ibid

participating in France's lust for aggrandizement." (MK, Vol II, p.471)

Lebensraum, Russia, and anti-Semitism

At and around the time of the Ruhr crisis, Hitler's speeches begin to take a more conciliatory tone with England. The reasons for this are complex, but they can be synthesised crudely as his growing anti-Semitism, his anti-communism, and renewed desire for German expansion. Despite fighting and defeating Russia during World War One, the two countries - having become international pariahs after the war - gravitated towards one another. This warming of relations is perhaps most clearly seen in the Treaty of Rapallo - whereby both countries agreed to renounce all territorial and pecuniary demands from one another as a result of the controversial Treaty of Brest-Litovsk in 1918. However, Hitler was largely unimpressed by this closeness. The Bolshevik Revolution had, in his eyes, been led entirely by Jews. Karl Marx, the father of Communism, was a Jew. As was Trotsky, Kamanev, Zinoviev and, most crucially for Hitler, Lenin. To Hitler, the consequences of the revolution, "...are that Russia is completely doomed to famine and misery, and responsible for all of this are the Jews!... Hopefully the German people will come to its senses and fight the Jews"[25].

Conflating the Russian Revolution with his rabid anti-Semitism, Hitler became convinced that the very future security of the German people depended upon the destruction of both. Into this mix was tossed Hitler's growing belief that the German people not only needed security and racial management, but also space. *Living space*, to be precise. The belief that the population of Germany had become so large that it literally

---

[25] Read, C. (1997) *The Evolution of Adolf Hitler's Weltanschauung: A Critical Study of His Rhetoric*. P.47. Massey University.

needed more space to exist fruitfully, increasingly became one of his non-negotiable stances. To acquire this Lebensraum, Hitler looked to the east, particularly to Poland. If Hitler, once in power, decided that the German state should invade and occupy anywhere east of their own borders, especially Poland, then he could expect an immediate military response from the Soviet Union. Unless...

Hitler became increasingly convinced that his future plans for the east, not to mention those underpinned by racial purification, required the friendship of a country (preferably one with support from an empire) that would act as a check to potential Russian aggression, could assuage French concern, and was ruled, apparently, by a largely non-Jewish political class. England became, in the mind of Hitler (both in the mid to late 1920's, as well as most of the 1930's), the country whose friendship was desirable above all others:

> *"Taking these considerations as a starting-point, anyone who investigates the possibilities that exist for Germany to find allies must come to the conclusion that there remains no other way of forming an alliance except to approach England."* (MK, Vol II, p.472)

Hitler then shows just how vital he believes this potential relationship with England to be when, in Mein Kampf, he makes the case for limiting the anti-English propaganda directed by the German state and her population:

> *"We cannot hope to be taken very seriously if we indulge in long-range abuse and protests against England..."* (MK, Vol II, p.485)

Apparently, *Albion* was less *Perfidious* in the mind of Hitler at this juncture.

Hitler Changes his Mind (again): War with England

Hitler and the Nazi propaganda machine continued, right up until late 1938, to wax lyrical about the 'success' of an Aryan England that had managed to subdue, conquer, and exploit so many of the world's peoples, collecting them into an empire unrivalled in history. When it became clear that Britain would never ally itself with Nazi Germany, something that was in abundant evidence at the Munich Conference in October, at which British Prime Minister Neville Chamberlain ceded part of Czechoslovakia (the Sudetenland) to Hitler, the decision was made to invert the policy of positive evangelism towards England and return to the dogma of *Perfidious Albion*. From this point onwards, the propaganda machinery of the Nazi state begins cranking out criticisms of England. The British Empire becomes evidence of worldwide oppression - and a weapon with which to counter British claims of minority oppression in Nazi Germany. The 'Aryan ruling class' of England became puppets of Jewish plutocrats and Bolsheviks with links to a global socialist Semite conspiracy to dominate the world.

Picture 18: German propaganda piece from 1 November 1940, blaming Neville Chamberlain for the war.

In a speech at Wilhelmshaven on April 1st, 1939, Hitler essentially laid out his reasoning for war (he called it 'defence') by explaining that England, along with a number of other countries, had fallen "...under the Jewish Bolshevist pest..." and that Germany, if it is not to suffer the same fate, must "...defend itself"[26].

Thus, we see how Hitler's 'very definite' opinion of England mutated, evolved, and contradicted itself, but always at the service of his wider ambitions. Perfidious Albion? Sometimes.

WHAT YOU DIDN'T KNOW WILL BLOW YOUR MIND

Land of the Angles

Hitler's affinity for the English (well, some of them) was partly derived from, what he saw, as a shared ancestry. The word 'England' owes its heritage to the Angles, who were a German tribe - probably from a region of Germany called *Anglia* - that came to England in the post-Roman era. *Angle-Land* - or Land of the Angles - became, over time, England. Thus, Hitler reasoned, there was a shared racial and cultural identity between Germany and England. This was sufficient for him to see a future where the two countries - shorn of their 'undesirable elements' - would become melded together. When discussing the power and success of the British Empire he was, in part, imagining that power as a proof of Germany's own power.

Directive Number 16/Unternehmen Seelöwe

On the 16 July 1940, a directive was issued from the Führer Headquarters which called for the attack, invasion, and occupation of England (not Great Britain, but England). This

---

[26] Speech to be found at http://hitler.org/speeches/04-01-39.html

was *Directive No. 16 On Preparations for a Landing Operation Against England* (Hitler issued a total of 74 such war-related directives). The 'cover' name for this operation was 'Seelöwe', or 'Sealion', the initial preparatory phase of which called for the destruction of the 'English Air Force'. This of course would culminate in the Battle of Britain - which the Nazis would lose, thus thwarting Hitler's plans for the domination of England.

SS Black Book

In September 1945, four months after the Allied defeat of Nazi Germany, a handbook marked 'secret' and titled *Informationsheft GB* was recovered from Berlin. The handbook had been created by the *Reich Main Security Office* (RHSA) - the head of which was, at the time of the book's creation, Reinhard Heydrich, the man whose name would go on to become synonymous with the prosecution of the Holocaust. The book was designed to support the German troops during Operation Sealion and contained maps of England, local geography, important landmarks, centres of civil administration, military locations and such. A supplement to this book was the *Sonderfahndungsliste G.B.*, or the *'Special Wanted List G.B.'* This list contained hundreds of names of notable British residents who were to be rounded up and imprisoned during the invasion. Included on this list of 2820 names, were obvious ones such as Winston Churchill and Clement Attlee, but there were some that were, perhaps more surprising. Virginia Woolf, H.G. Wells, Sylvia Pankhurst, Noël Coward, Sigmund Freud, and E.M. Forster all found themselves, much to their surprise, on this list. The book became known, rather dramatically, as the *SS Black Book*. Only two copies appear to have survived the bombing of the storage facility in Germany, one of which is housed in the Imperial War Museum of London.

291
Z

1. Zagorski, Wojczech, 2.9.07 Kozmin, Poln. N.-Agent, RSHA IV E 5.
2. Zaks, Julijs, brit. N.-Agent, richtig: Julius Sack (Täterkreis: Sudakoff), RSHA IV E 4.
3. Zaleska, Zofia, Mitgl. d. poln. Reg., RSHA IV D 2.
4. Zaleski, August, Außenmin., Mitgl. d. poln. Reg., RSHA IV D 2.
5. Zapf, Franz, 22.2.93 Wintersgrün, London. RSHA IV A 1 b.
6. Zapf, Robert, 16.12.90 Dogiasgrün, Krs. Elbogen, Sheffield, 147 Rustlings Road, RSHA IV A 1.
7. Zassenhaus, Herbert Kurt, Dr., geb. 1910, Dozent, London, Emigrant, RSHA III A 1.
8. Zeimer, Arthur, fr. Abraham, 16.10.77 Podwolczieka, Hptm., poln. N.-Agent, RSHA IV E 5, Stapoleit München.
9. Zeitler, Hans, 3.9.12 Hamburg, Wehrpflichtiger, zuletzt: Südafrika, vermutl. England, RSHA V D 2.
10. Zeligowski, Lucjan, General, Mitgl. d. poln. Nat.-Rat, RSHA IV D 2.
11. Zernatto, Guido, 21.7.03 Treffen, Schriftsteller, England, RSHA IV A 3.
12. Zernick, Rufin Rudolf, 7.3.01 Nicolai, poln. O. S., Kaufmann, poln. N.-Agent, RSHA IV E 5.
13. Zernike, J., Dr., zuletzt: Holland, vermutl. England, RSHA IV E 4.
14. Zeuner, Friedrich, Dr., 1905, Privatdozent, Emigrant, Universität, London, RSHA III A 1.
15. Zeylmans, J. W., zuletzt: Zaandam/Holl., vermutl. England (Täterkreis: Breijnen), RSHA IV E 4.
16. Ziaja, Anton, 7.6.04 Beuthen/O.S., Kellner, poln. N.-Agent, RSHA IV E 5, Stapo Oppeln.
17. Ziaja, Gerhardt, 4.9.13 Antonienhütte, Musiker, RSHA IV E 5, Stapo Oppeln.
18. Zibrid, Anton, 9.7.96 Graslitz, Margate-Kent, Northdown Road, RSHA IV A 1 b.
19. Ziehm, Alfred, 10.2.96 Dresden, Gewerkschafter, RSHA IV A 1 b.
20. von Zilfhout, J., zuletzt: Holland, vermutl. England, RSHA IV E 4, Stapo Bremen.
21. Zimmern, Alfred, 1879, Professor, RSHA VI G 1.
22. Zingler, Alfred, 6.6.85 Sprottau, Redakteur, vermutl. England, RSHA IV A 1.
23. Zinner, Josef, 27.3.94 Janessen, England, RSHA IV A 1 b.
24. Zowanski, Generalkonsul, RSHA IV D 2.
25. Zucker, Arthur, 21.7.94 Berlin, Redakteur, London, RSHA IV A 1.
26. Zuckermayer, Karl, 27.12.96 Nackenheim, London, Schriftsteller, Emigrant, RSHA VI G 1, II B 5.
27. van Zuiden, Ph., zuletzt: Baarn/Holl., vermutl. England (Täterkreis: Breijnen), RSHA IV E 4.
28. Zuniz, Leonie, Dr., geb. 1906, Emigrantin, Oxford (Universität), RSHA III A 1.
29. Zwart, Adrianus Johannes Josephus, 16.11.93 Loon op Zand, brit. N.-Agent, richtig: Vrinten, zuletzt: Rotterdam, vermutl. England (Täterkreis: Stevens/Best), RSHA IV E 4.
30. Zweig, Konrad, Dr., 1904, Assistent, Emigrant, London, RSHA III A 1.
31. Zweig, Stefan, Dr., 28.11.81 Wien (Jude), Schriftsteller, Emigrant, London W. 1, 49 Hallam Street, RSHA II B 2, II B 5, VI G 1.
32. Zychon, Jan Henryk, 1.1.96 Krakau, Kapitän, RSHA IV E 5.

Picture 19: A page from the SS 'Black Book'.

Hitler's 'visit' to Liverpool

Adolf Hitler's half-brother, Alois Hitler jr, moved to Liverpool from Dublin with his Irish wife, Bridget Dowling, in 1910. There they lived at 102 Upper Stanhope Street, in Toxteth and had a son they named William Patrick Hitler (ironically, this house would be destroyed in 1942 by the Nazi Luftwaffe). The couple split when Alois left abruptly for Germany in 1914. Bridget would later write a manuscript entitled, *My Brother-in-*

Law Adolf, in which she would claim that, in an attempt to evade Austrian military service, Adolf Hitler - her now world-famous brother in law - had visited the home she shared with Alois in Liverpool. This claim (largely debunked by historians) gained popular attention when Beryl Bainbridge published her fictional novel, *Young Adolf,* in 1978. Bainbridge had Hitler drinking in local pubs (*Peter Kavanagh's*) and getting into scrapes with locals. Despite their fanciful nature, the claims of Bridget Dowling have entered the pantheon of popular Liverpool mythology, persisting through the decades. Nonetheless, the very fact that Hitler had a brother in the Albion that he attempted at times to both woo *and* destroy, is of sufficient significance for it to be included in this chapter.

A Nazi Blackpool

In 2009, Michael Cole, a publisher in York, made public the fact that he had come into the possession of a large number of German maps from World War Two. Many of these maps detailed the Fylde coast in the west of England - home to the Lancashire holiday resort of Blackpool. During the war, the Nazi Luftwaffe had dropped thousands of tons of ordinance on strategic locations in England. Blackpool, one of England's more famous seaside tourist resorts, popular for its piers, sea air, pleasure gardens and tower, was also home to factories at Stanley Park Aerodrome and Squires Park which produced Vickers Wellington bombers. New Air Force recruits were trained at one of the four airfields, and the bombers, once produced, were used in the bombing of strategic locations in Germany. Not only this, but the resort was popular for returning British soldiers, was home to thousands of evacuees and civil servants having relocated from London, and was a key element in maintaining the morale of the public - many of whom saw Blackpool as a beacon of normalcy in a time of national disturbance, since tourism in the town carried on regardless. One would think that, outside of the major urban-industrial centres of Britain, Blackpool would warrant serious attention from Nazi bombers. This attention never transpired in the same way that it had for other parts of the country.

One reason put forward for this is the so called 'People's Playground' - the suggestion that Hitler had deliberately spared the seaside resort so that it might serve as the recreation resort of the SS and other high-ranking Nazis. From the documents discovered by Michael Cole - including detailed aerial maps of the piers, the tower and the parks, it has been concluded by some that Hitler wanted to drop paratroopers into Stanley Park and march his men up and down the coastline during Operation Sealion. As part of the 'Blackpool as Nazi Pleasure Town' narrative, Hitler was very keen on the place and had deliberately ordered that it be spared from harm (although some bombing did take place). Having said this, Michael Cole argues that this notion is mixing correlation with causation. Nonetheless, if you want to see just how far and wide this story is accepted as true, a simple Google search would suffice.

Nazi Sabotage in the Isle of Wight?

Ever since the curtain came down on the European theatre of World War Two, Britain has proudly and patriotically upheld the popular narrative that its geographical integrity was never breached by the shoes of German invaders (excepting the Channel Islands). However, this popular recounting of national resistance in Britain's darkest hour was recently questioned by author Adrian Searle. Searle published a book in 2016, *Churchill's Last Wartime Secret: The 1941 German Raid Airbrushed from History*, in which he revealed evidence that the Nazis had in fact landed on the Isle of Wight.

Four miles off the south coast of mainland Britain and boasting four airfields, the Isle of Wight may have made a perfect base of operations from which the Nazis could project their power during Operation Sealion. In fact, according to military historian, Dr Robert Forczyk, Hitler had suggested doing just that. According to Forczyk's research of German military records, he suggests in his book, *We March Against England: Operation Sealion, 1940-41*, that Hitler was persuaded not to occupy the Isle of Wight by his Naval Commanders who believed it was too heavily defended by the British. It wasn't particularly, but it did have an RAF radar station called St. Lawrence.

Picture 20: RAF St Lawrence, was this, now buried, CH radar site the target of a secret Nazi mission on the Isle of Wight?

According to Searle, and supported by first-hand German evidence and local testimony, it was to this radar station that the Nazis turned their attention on August 15, 1943. It was on this day a Nazi soldier - one Dr Dietrich Andernacht - would later record that he and 11 other specialised troops landed on the Isle of Wight in dinghies, having paddled from U-boats that had made their way secretly to the coastline. They were engaged by British soldiers, rather than the expected Home Guard, but were able to make their way to the radar station, which they searched for 'cathode ray direction finding equipment'. Despite the Air Raid Precaution logbook on the Isle of Wight noting the event, all other evidence was, according to Searle, destroyed on the orders of Churchill in the name of maintaining morale. However, local testimony still maintains that a number of islanders were forced to sign the Official Secrets Act very shortly after the 15th August 1943 - testimony which wholly undermines the British wartime narrative of an impenetrable bastion. It also, if true, gives us insight into Hitler's view of *Perfidious Albion,* right up to the latter stages of World War Two: that of a country occupying, in a profound way, both his mind and his designs.

4

HAPPINESS AND THE HAKENKREUZ: HOW EVERYBODY USED TO LOVE THE SWASTIKA

WHAT YOU NEED TO KNOW

In 1920, the National Socialist German Workers' Party adopted, what would become, the most identifiable symbol of any political party in history (including the hammer and sickle of communist parties around the world): the black swastika embedded in a white circle against a red background. Adolf Hitler, in Mein Kampf, claimed to have single-handedly created the insignia:

> *"I myself was always for keeping the old colours...After innumerable trials I decided upon a final form – a flag of red material with a white disc bearing in its centre a black swastika. After many trials I obtained the correct proportions between the dimensions of the flag and of the white central disc, as well as that of the swastika. And this is how it has remained ever since."* (MK, Vol II, p.383)

Picture 21: The swastika flag of the Nazi Party

Rotated 45 degrees, with the 'hooks' of the black cross falling clockwise, the swastika or, as it was known in German, the hakenkreuz (hooked cross), was initially limited in its use to the party's regalia: the badge, armband and flag. However, after 1933, it became nearly ubiquitous across Germany, ultimately being adopted as the country's flag. The flag would then go on to be flown across much of Europe. Many people are aware of the fact that the swastika has a long and rich history of use across parts of Asia; what most people don't know is that, prior to World War Two, the swastika was as ubiquitous as any symbol across western Europe and the United States – used in a multitude of ways from advertising campaigns to insignia on USAF planes during World War One.

Picture 22: The second American woman to earn a pilot's licence, Matilde E. Moisant, pictured in 1912. Notice the swastika – for good luck.

WHY IT'S IMPORTANT THAT YOU KNOW THIS

In the early morning of May 20th, 1927, Charles Lindbergh lifted the nose of his Ryan Airlines manufactured *Spirit of St. Louis* from the grass of Roosevelt Airfield, New York, beginning a journey that would go down in history as the first successful non-stop solo Atlantic crossing and make Lindbergh and his aircraft American legends. Eight days earlier, *Spirit of St. Louis* developed a dangerous crack just behind its propeller. Lindbergh was forced to replace the propeller and its nose cone. Inside the nose cone there were a number of names of people who had signed it for good luck. These signatures belonged to some of those men and women responsible for the construction of the plane, such as B. F. Mahoney - the president of Ryan Airlines. Dead centre of the nose cone, and surrounded by the names of these pioneering Americans, a large, bold swastika had been scribed. As counterfactual as it may be, had the nose cone not been replaced eight days before the history-making flight, the first thing of this profoundly American adventure to enter French airspace on the 21st May, would have been a swastika.

The team that built *Spirit of St. Louis* were not Nazis. Although Lindbergh himself moved towards the right of American politics in the 1930's, he could never honestly be described as a fascist. In fact, the swastika inside the nose cone of the legendary aircraft was a good luck symbol. This historic scribbling was not representative of any form of authoritarianism. It was, in truth, emblematic of a fashionable trend in the western world at this time: to use the swastika as a symbol of good luck. This trend was so widespread and popular, that the swastika became prolific across Western Europe and the United States. From soap to cough sweets, the swastika adorned the advertising campaigns of companies throughout the early decades of the twentieth century.

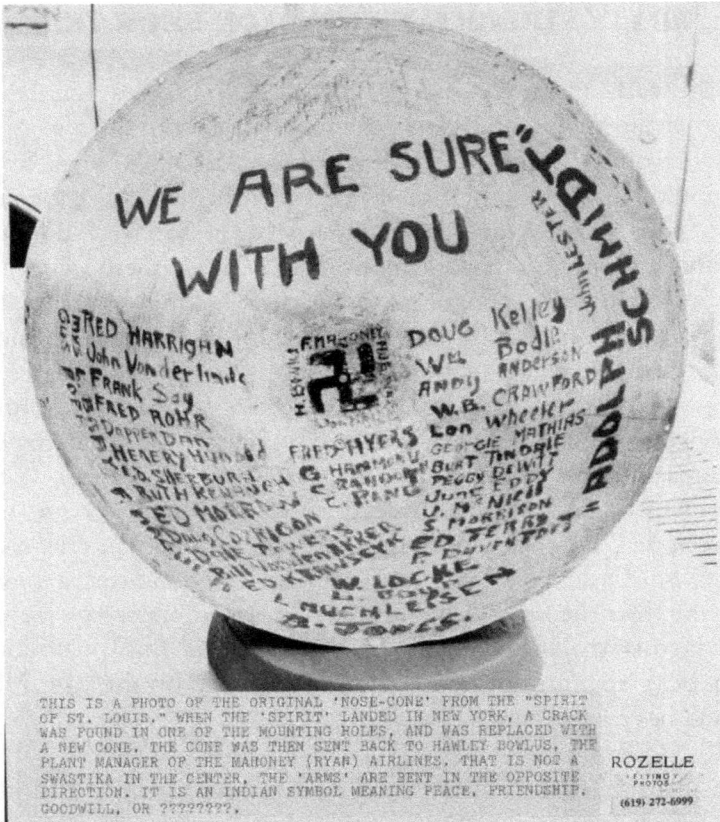

Picture 22: Inside the original nosecone of Spirit of St. Louis

Of course, the swastika has a much deeper history than this - something we shall explore in the course of the chapter - but the staggering reality is that the symbol which has come to so immediately represent horror, racism, and fear was, right up until the terror of the Nazis became apparent, a nearly ubiquitous and positive image in those countries that would come so close to destruction by those who 'stole' it. What is perhaps more staggering, is that it's early twentieth century usage in the West, has been largely forgotten by history.

WHAT THIS IS CONNECTED TO

The Nazi Party: A small boat in a sea of ships

In the years immediately following World War One, there were a number of specific challenges confronting the political parties of Germany. Among the many of these challenges were some that were more pressing than others: how would a party differentiate itself from all of the others competing for power? It's important to remember that, after the abdication of the Kaiser and under the new Weimar Constitution, political parties of all persuasions had proliferated across Germany at an unprecedented rate of birth. In the 1919 federal elections, for example, there were 19 parties vying for seats in the Reichstag. How would a political party spread its, often complicated, agenda successfully to the masses - in short, what did each party represent? Perhaps even more importantly, who were the people that each party was trying to target and how would they target them? Germany was awash in a sea of political, social and economic chaos - how would a party cut through the chaos and reach out to the people and unify them? The answer came in the form of the red and white flag with the bold black swastika at its heart. The swastika distilled into the simplest terms, what the National Socialists stood for. In order to understand what it was that they stood for, and how the swastika became indelibly marked with the National Socialist ink, utterly inverting its original meaning, then read on.

The Herrenvolk

Adolf Hitler was a firm believer that the German people were somehow a 'chosen' people, destined to dominate the world by virtue of their superior bloodlines. The notion of Germans as somehow 'Übermenschen' (literally translated as *Overmen*, but more commonly as *Supermen*) had gained traction in German nationalist circles. In part, this was because of a misapplication of the ideas contained in the German philosopher Friedrich Nietzsche's *Thus Spoke Zarathustra*, by a trending eugenicism sweeping predominantly white parts of the world, and by German people looking for meaning after the decline of their imperial prestige. A mythology began to grow within Germany and other countries of northern Europe at the time, that their peoples were directly descended from a group of Indo-Europeans known as *Aryans*, and that somehow this group represented a superior classification of Caucasians. That Germany was left defeated and ruined by World War One was explained by many with a mind to do so within Germany, as a result of betrayal and conspiracy, but also as a result of a dilution of the nation's superior *Aryan* bloodlines. A common trope of nationalist political parties looking for power was that they could restore German pride - something that had been lost after 1918 - by returning the mythical 'herrenvolk' or 'master race' to their rightful position: that of the dominators of others.

The swastika was chosen by Hitler (and many others within Germany at the time) because of a number of convenient coincidences and deliberate conflations which happened to support their narrative of a restoration of the *Aryan* 'herrenvolk'. While avoiding the historical 'sin' of mono causation, perhaps the single greatest assist in 'proving' this narrative, was the discovery by clumsy German archaeologist Heinrich Schliemann of swastika symbols at the ancient city of Troy. He erroneously connected these symbols with similar ones found on ancient German pots and concluded, as many others enthusiastically also did, that the ancient Greeks and the ancient Germans were racially and culturally connected, thus 'proving' their genealogical superiority to other European races. Consequently, in concert with a number of other developments, the völkisch movements of the early twentieth century began adopting the swastika as 'proof' of the Germanic 'herrenvolk' - very much a new development in the history of the symbol.

Picture 23: Heinrich Schliemann (top right) at Lion Gate, Mykene. Excavating 'Troy'

The propaganda of history

Needless to say, the swastika was central to the propaganda machinery of the National Socialists. Regardless of the abominable messages with which the symbol became associated later - after Hitler's consolidation of his authority (1933-34) - the red flag with the white circle, at the centre of which was the 'crooked cross', contained deliberate and recognisable meaning to many Germans. It was this meaning that the Nazi propaganda machinery was developed to celebrate and propagate: German history (the red, white, and black were the three colours of the flag of imperial Germany), the social dimension of National Socialist principles (the red), a powerful nationalism (the white), and the supposed racial purity and superiority of the German people (the black swastika).

Writing in Volume II of Mein Kampf, Hitler wrote the following:

> *"...it incorporated those revered colours expressive of our homage to the glorious past and which once brought so much honour to the German nation, but this symbol was also an eloquent expression of the will behind the movement. We National Socialists regarded our flag as being the embodiment of our party programme. The red expressed the social thought underlying the movement. White the national thought. And the swastika signified the mission allotted to us – the struggle for the victory of Aryan mankind and at the same time the triumph of the ideal of creative work which is in itself and always will be anti-Semitic."* (MK, Vol II, p.384)

The centrality of the swastika to the creation of a Nazi mythology can be seen in the controversial but brilliant propaganda film, *Triumph of the Will* (Triumph des Willens) by Leni Riefenstahl, which immortalised the 1935 Nazi Party Rally in Nuremberg on celluloid. Not only is there a swastika in practically every shot, the *very first* shot is of an iron eagle atop a swastika.

With these meanings enshrined so overtly in the flag of the Nazi Party, once the Party became the dominant force in German Politics and the flag flew everywhere (on the 15th September 1935 the Nazi flag became the official flag of Germany) and was emblazoned on everything, the principles of Nazism would be instantly understood and practically inescapable. If Hitler was not always visible to Germans, the swastika would represent him. This, patently, was about as far away from the swastika's fashionable twentieth century meaning as it was possible to get. People outside of Germany began, in the main, to despise - not love - the swastika.

The Nuremberg Laws

At the annual NSDAP rally held at Nuremberg in September 1935, a set of laws known collectively as the Nuremberg Laws (see later chapter) effectively wrote Germany's Jews out of the German constitution and classified them as a racial demographic rather than a religious one. The effects of these laws are explored later in this book in more depth, but they effectively laid the legal foundation for much of the persecution that would fall upon the Jews of Germany and Europe. On the same day as the Nuremberg Laws targeting the Jewish community in Germany were expediently passed, another law came into being: the Reich Flag Law. As mentioned above, this law made the Nazi flag the German flag. It is in keeping with the racial messages contained within the Nazi flag, that a law introducing it as the symbol of the country be passed in the same tranche of racist legislation targeting the Jewish community of Germany. The law even forbade Jews from raising the new flag or displaying its colours.

Killing the swastika

The symbol of the swastika is a victim of recent history. Before it was co-opted by the Nazis and turned into a symbol of hate and racism, the swastika could be found throughout the world and the historical record, usually representing such things as auspiciousness, good fortune, the sun and its movements, rebirth, creation, the universe, and life. Most people are reasonably familiar with the Asiatic incarnations of the swastika - the word itself derives from the Sanskrit word *svastika*, meaning, among other things, 'well-being' and 'good luck'. The symbol has a history spanning thousands of years of meaning and usage to Hindus but is also deeply entrenched in the histories of other cultures and societies. For Buddhists all across Asia, the swastika continues to be used as a symbol of prosperity, eternity and good fortune; Christians have used the symbol from Rome (in the Christian catacombs) to Ethiopia (at the site of the orthodox rock-cut churches of Lalibela); Native American tribes across North America employed the design throughout their histories; Nordic peoples have illustrated their mythology with swastikas for hundreds of years. The picture below, of the present-day Washington County Court House in Ohio, is an example of the symbol's twentieth century usage.

Picture 24: Past and present converge. The second floor of the Washington County Court House, Ohio, today. The floor was created long before the Nazis took the swastika as their own.

This list of histories engraved with the symbol of the swastika is wide-ranging - both geographically and temporally - but they all seem to be united by their view of the symbol as something positive. Although there can be a duality to the swastika, for example a 'reversed' swastika can have an adverse meaning to Hindus, often encompassing violence and death, it always seems to represent a formal type of righteous justice. The Goddess of Kali may be invoked by the 'reversed' swastika but, although she is sometimes depicted as the bringer of death, it is a death of man's ego, attachment to materialism, and tendency towards pettiness. In this sense, although she may cause death, she brings rebirth and purity. Thus, even the reversed swastika appears righteous. The reversed swastika of the Nazis contained no such righteousness of meaning.

WHAT YOU DIDN'T KNOW WILL BLOW YOUR MIND

In Germany, the swastika didn't belong to the Nazis

The Nazi Party were by no means the only political group in Germany that used the swastika for their own ends. Particularly after World War One, far right nationalist groups of all stripes within Germany adopted the swastika as a symbol of racial superiority and national pride. During the Kapp Putsch of March 1920, for example, a *Free Corps* (Freikorps) group called the *Marinebrigade Ehrhardt* fought alongside Wolfgang Kapp, displaying the Swastika. The swastika was not, even in post war Germany, the sole preserve of the Nazi.

Picture 25: The Marinebrigade Ehrhardt during the Kapp Putsch. Notice the swastikas on the front and side of the truck.

How events in America helped to turn the Nazi flag into the German flag

There is an argument to be made that the Nazis adopted the swastika as their national flag - thus ensuring both its proliferation across Europe and its historical infamy - because of the Americans. In 1935, a German liner - the SS Bremen - was docked in New York Harbor, at the North German Lloyd shipping company's pier, and quickly became the focus of Americans looking to protest anti-Semitic, anti-Catholic, and anti-communist developments in Germany. On the 26th July, a group of people stormed the liner, tore the swastika from its bow and dumped it in the Hudson River, to the loud 'hurrahs' of the onlookers. The man who tore the flag from the jackstaff was Bill Bailey (see his *The Kid from Hoboken: An Autobiography*). Perhaps inspired by this action, similar 'flag-ripping' protests occurred around the world. When Hans Luther, the German Ambassador to the US, complained to the American government about the destruction of the flag, the reply was that the swastika was merely the symbol of the National Socialist Party and NOT of the country, therefore no international transgression had taken place. In response to the perceived desecration of the swastika, the Reich Flag Law was passed at Nuremberg in September 1935. This made the swastika the official flag of Germany. This simultaneously killed any notion of a return to the Weimar days and, perhaps more importantly, meant that all future demonstrations against the flag would be demonstrations against Germany, not merely the political party ruling it.

Swastika: History & Fashion

Perhaps the earliest depiction of the swastika was found in Mezine, Ukraine. Dated to around 15,000 BC, a swastika pattern on a figurine of a bird appears to be the oldest example we have so far discovered. Of particular interest to this author (born, as I was, in the north of England) is, what most archaeologists consider to be, a Bronze Age swastika carved in a stone in Ilkley Moor in Yorkshire. The 'Ilkley Moor Swastika' appears to be entirely unique in the whole of England.

Despite its apparently prehistoric roots, the swastika saw something of a renaissance in the West towards the end of the 19th and the beginning of the 20th century. This revival of the symbol was in keeping with the profound positivity carried in its ancient meanings - used to promote good luck and well-being. In her piece for BBC Magazine entitled *How the world loved the swastika - until Hitler stole it*, Mukti Jain Campion details some of the surprising places the swastika was to be found before it was adopted by the National Socialists. In one example, Campion explains how the swastika "...was used by American military units during World War One..." and that the RAF had planes embossed with the swastika "...as late as 1939[27]". Others, such as the leading authority on graphic design, Steven Heller, who published a book titled: *The Swastika: Symbol Beyond Redemption?*, examined the history of the symbol - by way of some startling examples of its use, such as by Coca Cola.

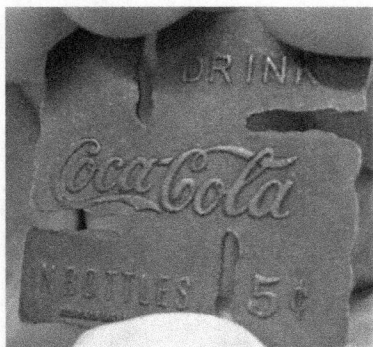

Picture 26: Part of a Coca Cola key fob from the 1920's.

[27] Campion, Mukti Jain. (2014) *How the world loved the swastika – until Hitler stole it.* Available at: https://www.bbc.com/news/magazine-29644591 (Accessed: August 2018)

Examples of the twentieth century 'fashion' for employing the swastika as a good luck symbol can be seen from Russia to Finland. The swastika adorned some of the bank notes printed and used by the Provisional Government of Russia, once Tsar Nicholas had abdicated the throne. The Finnish Air Force used a blue swastika as its emblem from 1918-45, and it can still be seen on unit flags and insignia today. Although controversial, the use of the swastika in modern day Finland can be traced back to the Iron Age. It wound up as the symbol of the Finnish Air Force because of an early twentieth century Swedish aviator who painted his aircraft with a good luck symbol: a blue swastika. He would later gift one of his planes to the White Forces of Finland - which became the air force's first aircraft. From this point onwards, until 1945, the planes of the Finnish Air Force carried the large blue swastika.

Picture 27: Finnish Air Force plane during World War Two

Picture 28: Insignia of the Finnish Air Force Karelia Air Command. Designed by Olof Eriksson, approved by the President of Finland in 1957.

Rudyard Kipling, the legendary author of such works as *The Jungle Book*, frequently employed the swastika as art on the covers and interiors of his books - long before the Nazis employed it for their own designs. For example, on the cover of his book of poems, *The Five Nations,* published in 1903, Kipling employs a swastika alongside an elephant (representing the Hindu God, Ganesh).

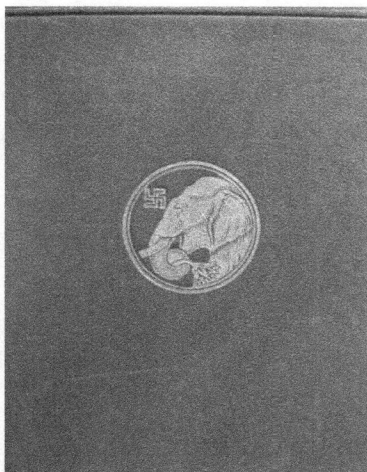

Picture 29: Front cover of one of Rudyard Kipling's many books

ALL RIGHTS RESERVED INCLUDING THAT OF TRANSLATION
INTO FOREIGN LANGUAGES, INCLUDING THE SCANDINAVIAN

COPYRIGHT, 1909, BY RUDYARD KIPLING
PUBLISHED OCTOBER, 1909

Picture 30: Inside of Rudyard Kipling's 1909 book, Actions and Reactions

In his wonderful book, Steven Heller also places the Nazi appropriation of the swastika in a wider historical context - showing its consistent usage through time and geography - in order to pose the question of whether it can ever be rehabilitated away from the National Socialists. The question is a poignant one that is currently being discussed by socialists, historians and religious groups. There are those who have already made their decision: November 13th is *'Learn to Love the Swastika Day'*. An event commemorating the work of artist 'ManWoman' who encouraged the world to reclaim the swastika and use it in its original contexts - of peace, rebirth and so on. On this date, tattoo parlours around the world offer free swastika tattoos to those taking part, in an attempt to deconstruct the Nazi meaning and reconstruct a more positive meaning.

Picture 31: The present-day flag of Kuna Yala

5

BREAKING OF THE BEEFSTEAK NAZIS: HITLER'S GREATEST ASSET AND HIS GREATEST THREAT

WHAT YOU NEED TO KNOW

As the National Socialist German Workers' Party grew beyond the confines of its earlier form (the largely insignificant German Workers' Party), and Hitler became its recognised, charismatic leader, so it became necessary to both demonstrate and protect its growing power. In the violent thuggery of early Weimar politics, successful parties began to employ paramilitaries that would double as security guards for their leaders as well as agitators to break up the meetings of other parties.

Initially, the people that would serve these two functions were former soldiers, and *Freikorps* members who supported the National Socialists. They appeared voluntarily at early meetings and, without organisation or instruction, would eject those that had come to cause disruption - usually Social Democrats and members of the German Communist Party (KPD). Almost organically, they became the de facto protectors/vigilantes for Hitler and the Party. Ever alive to propaganda and political opportunities as well as the need to project the appearance of organisation and power, not to mention the practical need for self-defence, Hitler decided to formalise what had grown almost naturally as an invaluable element of the Nazi Party. As a result, in 1921 the 'Storm Detachment', as it had become informally known, was *officially* named as such. Thus, the SA was born.

The 1920's were turbulent years for the Nazis and the SA, in part due to the Munich Putsch (after which the SA, or *Brown Shirts* as they became known, were outlawed), and in part due to the humiliating election of 1928, in which the NSDAP gained only 12 seats in the Reichstag. Despite these setbacks, the ranks of the SA (rebranded the *Frontbann* for a while in order to bypass the legal ban on their existence) swelled beyond anticipation. Ernst Röhm, the brutish leader of the SA, was a magnet for disaffected former soldiers. Despite Hitler and Röhm's frequent arguments (one in particular leading to Röhm's abrupt departure in 1928 for Bolivia, whereupon he was employed as a training advisor and Lieutenant Colonel for the nation's army), they would always reconcile. While in Bolivia, Hitler called Röhm directly to ask him to come back to Germany because he needed him. In the years 1929-33 the SA would play a role which, in the eyes of the *Führer*, was a prerequisite for the success of the Party. The SA and Ernst Röhm were so deeply embedded in the fabric of Hitler's vision for achieving power during the years of the Great Depression, that when Hitler became Chancellor in January 1933, many within the Party, including Röhm himself, believed that the traditional German army would naturally be absorbed into the SA - which at this point in time, had in excess of 3 million members. Let us not forget that the official *Reichswehr* was limited by the terms of the Treaty of Versailles to a mere 100,000 soldiers. Röhm's vision was, of course, not shared by Hitler - who had entirely different ideas. Why, exactly, Hitler did not share Ernst Röhm's post-1933 enthusiasm for an ascendant SA, had much to do with the need for the newly inaugurated chancellor to claim the support of the traditional military establishment of Germany. It also had much to with the very real danger of a 3 million-strong paramilitary operating under the loyal control of a man with whom he had had frequent and public disagreements. In addition to these core concerns, it also had much to do with the fact that many within the SA were *Beefsteak Nazis.*

WHY IT'S IMPORTANT THAT YOU KNOW THIS

Although in its early years the SA was viewed largely as a group of disorganised thugs looking for an outlet for their violent tendencies, it began to organise itself along military lines and became a well-drilled behemoth of power and discipline, albeit with a well-earned reputation for brutality. In the uncertain times of Weimar, particularly after the collapse of the global economy triggered by the Wall Street Crash, the SA projected a choreographed stability and organisation - a stark contrast to the chaos ravaging much of Germany. In a time of rampant unemployment, the SA even became a clear example of what the National Socialists could be in such dire times: an attractive employer. To those with a mind to see it as such, the SA became a beacon of order as well as a reminder of the success that German authoritarianism could bring. In short, the SA, for all of its obvious failings, was an invaluable weapon of Nazi propaganda and an incisive instrument of political surgery. Unfortunately, Röhm saw the role of the ever-expanding military wing of the NSDAP as more than a mere tool to *gain* power; he saw it as a revolutionary force that would *become* power. Unlike Hitler, who rejected the importance of socialism within the Party programme, seeing it primarily as a means of attracting workers away from KPD and not as an ideological promise for the future, Röhm believed that his SA would be the vanguard of a socialist workers revolution that would be constructed once the Nazis had gained power. Revolution, of a socialist and working-class kind, was Röhm's Raison d'être. By natural extension, it was also that of his Brownshirts. Counter-intuitively, for one of the most notoriously brutal *right-wing* paramilitaries in modern history, there is substantial evidence to suggest that the vast majority of the 3 million the SA counted among its ranks by 1934, were communists and socialists.

According to a number of historians, including Konrad Heiden[28], many within the SA ranks were known as *Beefsteak Nazis:* brown on the outside, red on the inside. This most likely comes as something of a revelation to many, bearing in mind Hitler despised communism and was largely disinterested in the working classes beyond their production and voting capacities.

Many of the falling outs that Röhm had with Hitler centred around his ongoing concerns that the promise of a socialist workers revolution which had embedded itself within the dogma of the SA rank and file and had attracted so many of them into the organisation in the first place, needed to become reality. Hitler and other high-ranking Nazis would frequently flatter Röhm into submission, intimating that the role of the SA was crucial for the success of the party, but stymieing any suggestion that a revolution, the kind of which their SA members were looking for, would transpire any time soon. "Wait, wait, soon..." seemed to be the response to Röhm's desire for immediate socialist revolution. Of course, this could never become a reality, and Hitler knew it. One of the reasons for the removal of Ernst Röhm in the *Night of the Long Knives*[29], was because he had promoted a vision of the SA after Hitler had assumed power in 1933, as spearheading a second revolution that would secure the future of both the SA and the country's working classes. This terrified the German *Reichswehr* (the traditional German Military) and the business interests that had invested heavily in Hitler's success.

Once Hitler was in power, the SA became a political liability because of Röhm's insistence that the SA should absorb the traditional German army (the Reichswehr) and become the official military of Nazi Germany. However, once Röhm and

---

[28] Heiden, K. (1938). *Hitler: A Biography.* England. Constable & Co., Ltd
[29] The Night of the Long Knives refers to the purging of the SA leadership in 1934, something discussed in depth later in this chapter.

other high-ranking SA leaders had been purged in the Night of the Long Knives, the SA took something of a back seat in terms of their importance. The SS and the Reichswehr became the dominant military forces in the country. However, that's not to say the SA were a spent force - they were continually used in propaganda - particularly aimed at younger German men. The proud, athletic and, now respectable, stormtroopers became, in many respects, the very embodiment of the völkisch evangelism emanating from Goebbels' Ministry of Propaganda.

Picture 32: Röhm (front right) and Hitler

WHAT THIS IS CONNECTED TO

The Bamberg Conference

As discussed more fully in a later chapter, the Bamberg Conference, which took place in 1926 on the request of the newly-released-from-prison Hitler, was a meeting of the nation's Nazi Party leaders. The main goal of the conference, as Hitler saw it, was to unite the party after the fractures and fissures opened up by the failed Munich Putsch[30] had threatened its very existence and Hitler's leadership of it. For Hitler, unity meant that the party should coalesce permanently around his ideological vision and his authority as their Führer. A clear schism - both geographically and ideologically - ran through the conference. The northern, urban leadership comprised of such men as Joseph Goebbels, Gregor Strasser, and Ernst Röhm. These promoted a vision of the Party as socialist, working class and revolutionary. The southern, rural leadership of Gottfried Feder and Hitler rejected urban socialist revolution in favour of rural, racialist-infused populism. Right here, as early as 1926 - well before the SA had collected nearly 3 million acolytes - we see the point at which Hitler and Röhm's futures diverged. Hitler's rejection of the NSDAP as a socialist workers party of revolution at the Bamberg Conference is a tacit acknowledgement of just how deeply ingrained within the Party socialism and the rights of workers had become. Hitler's very leadership of the Nazis was under direct threat at Bamberg; had he failed to turn the significant number of leaders away from their goals of socialist revolution, both the Party and Hitler would have been done for. Even Goebbels, the man who would go on to become Hitler's most fanatical loyalist, noted in his diary after the conference that Hitler's rejection of socialist revolution was "...probably one of the greatest disappointments of my life. I no longer believe

---

[30] You will remember from earlier in the book that the Munich Putsch was Hitler's attempt to seize power in Bavaria in 1923

fully in Hitler"[31]. It should therefore come as little surprise that one of the men so keenly protective of such a socialist future, would not abandon it easily. Röhm would abandon it even less easily, once he had the power of 3 million *Beefsteak Nazis* at his disposal.

End of the Socialist Workers Revolution: Operation Hummingbird

Students of History might be familiar with the Night of the Long Knives - the night upon which Ernst Röhm and other SA leaders were purged from the party. What many are less familiar with, is the reasoning behind it and its links to 'Beefsteak Nazism'.

Increasingly after Hitler's ascent to the Chancellery in January 1933, Röhm and the SA leadership had been agitating for the completion of their socialist mission: a second revolution in the name of Germany's workers. The agitation had become a political danger and a public embarrassment to Hitler, who was deeply concerned by Röhm's pronouncements that the SA would lead a 'second revolution' in the name of socialism and the workers. In the wider context of Hitler's consolidation of power in the months immediately following his appointment as Chancellor of Germany, any mention of the word 'revolution', let alone a socialist one looking to 'release' industrial workers from their business-owning oppressors, threatened to destabilise the fragile coalition of the military establishment, traditional German nationalists, and the country's industrialists, that Hitler had so carefully brought together. Hitler had decided back at the Bamberg Conference (if not earlier) that socialism was a barrier to power and not the aim of it. Compounding this was the all-pervading fear of communism

---

[31] Goebbels, J. (19th January 1929). Diary Entry. Available at: https://spartacus-educational.com/GERsa.htm (Accessed: July 2018)

that was driving the power-owning interests of Germany towards a return to authoritarianism. If Hitler was being forced to choose between his own leadership and his loyal old friend, there was no choice: the 'Beefsteak Nazis' would have to go. All 3 million of them.

In the early morning of the 30th June 1934, Hitler arrived in a motorcade of armed SS men at the lobby of Hanselbauer Hotel in the municipality of Bad Wiessee, Upper Bavaria. Two days earlier, Hitler had called Röhm and told him to convene a meeting of the SA leadership at this hotel. Röhm, perhaps thinking that Hitler wished to discuss future plans for the SA, did as he was asked. On that morning, according to his chauffeur, Erich Kempka, Hitler found his way to Ernst Röhm's room and, carrying nothing more than a whip, strode through the entrance to it. Despite the propaganda that would later paint a scene of homosexual debauchery, Röhm was not with a lover. Barking that Röhm was under arrest, Hitler moved so that the two armed SS men behind him could take the prisoner into their custody. The rest of the SA leadership were rounded up and taken to the laundry of the hotel. From there, they were transported to Stadelheim Prison. Most of them were executed immediately.

Picture 33: Kurheim Hanselbauer Hotel, scene of the Night of the Long Knives.

Estimates vary from between 200-1000 people who were killed in the two days following that morning at the Hanselbauer Hotel. Hitler himself admitted to the execution of a much smaller number but, for weeks after, bodies were still being found scattered across Bavaria; most of them were not members of the SA. Röhm's ultimate fate was not sealed immediately, as initially Hitler decided to spare his old friend. However, under pressure from the likes of Himmler, Hitler agreed that Röhm posed too much of a threat while he lived. Despite being given a loaded pistol by the two SS men sent by Himmler to Stadelheim Prison - Theodor Eike and Michael Lippert - so that he might take his own life, Röhm refused, apparently demanding that Hitler himself should come to the prison to carry out the deed. After roughly ten minutes without a gunshot ringing out from Röhm's cell, the two men walked into it and brought the Beefsteak Nazi revolution to a definite and bloody end. Röhm was murdered in his Stadelheim Prison cell on the 1st July. Operation Hummingbird was the codename given to the sweeping and murderous purge of Röhm, the SA leadership, and whichever opponents Hitler had decided could be swept from their positions of power.

The Blutfahne: The Blood Flag

Despite the death of the SA as an independent and potent paramilitary force within Germany after Operation Hummingbird, they were not, by any stretch of the imagination, discarded. They were still very useful, both as an organisation and, almost more importantly, as a contrivance of propaganda - something they had, in fact, always been. Perhaps one of the more symbolic and deliberately emotive pieces of propaganda that originated with the SA and helped to build the Nazi tri-myth of struggle, sacrifice and blood, was the Blutfahne, or Blood Flag. When, during the attempted putsch of 1923, government soldiers and police exchanged fire in the Odeonsplatz of central Munich with the marching Nazis, a number of the SA were killed. Two members of the SA in particular came to play a central part in the future myth-building of the National Socialists: *Heinrich Trambauer* and *Andreas Bauriedl.* Trambauer carried the swastika flag of the 5th SA Sturm as they marched towards the Feldherrnhalle in the Odeonsplatz. As the shooting started, Trambauer was hit and he dropped the flag. Next to him was Bauriedl who, having been shot in the stomach, fell dead and bleeding upon the flag.

What happened to the flag immediately following the collapse of the putsch is a matter of speculation, but it turned up later in the possession of an SA activist, Karl Eggers, who gave it to Hitler upon his release from Landsberg Prison. The flag was left uncleaned and unrepaired but given a new staff and finial. Just below the finial atop the staff, a silver 'sleeve' carried a dedication to the sixteen Nazis who died during the putsch. These men now entered the mythology of National Socialism - they became 'martyrs' - and sacrifice became a cornerstone of its ideology. The blood of the 'martyrs' that ran through the fabric of the flag was used to powerful effect thereafter. Nazi ceremonies would often involve the 'anointing' of party flags with the Blutfahne - simply by touching them together. More than this, at Party rallies in Nuremberg, a ceremony called the *Fahnenweihe* (flag consecration), whereby Nazi banners would be 'sanctified' by the Blutfahne relic, was designated as an essential element of the high-profile proceedings. In this sense, the SA had provided Hitler with the genesis of a religious experience which drew consciously from the narratives of sacrifice, communion, and struggle embedded in most dominant faiths, not to mention the obvious racialism inherent in the purifying properties of Aryan blood. Though there was no 'second revolution' for the Beefsteaks Nazis, the Blutfahne was a potent reminder to anyone with a desire to see it, of the once-held and revolutionary ambitions of the SA. Hitler might have chosen not to see this reminder, but it persevered long after Röhm's death.

Picture 34: The Blutfahne riding with Hitler in 1935 through the streets of Nuremberg. One year after the murder of Ernst Röhm

WHAT YOU DIDN'T KNOW WILL BLOW YOUR MIND

A Vegetarian and a Beefsteak: A turbulent friendship

Despite Hitler ultimately ordering the execution of Ernst Röhm on the Night of the Long Knives, the two men were very close. Regardless of their many differences, a shared belief that the organisation of the NSDAP (the Nazi Party) should follow along military lines, as well as having a similar history of soldierly commitment during World War One, helped the pair develop a mutual respect for one another. Perhaps this was why, out of all the high-ranking Nazis, Röhm was the only one who dared call Hitler anything other than 'mein Führer'. It was perhaps this familiarity which also allowed for the blazing rows the two would occasionally have. Röhm often challenged Hitler in public and was known even to call him 'Adi'. Other Nazis were horrified and, in some cases, jealous of the familiarity that Röhm seemed to enjoy with Hitler. This jealousy would manifest itself in the ease with which other high-ranking Nazis - from Himmler to Göring - enthusiastically called for his execution on the Night of the Long Knives.

Picture 35: Hitler and Röhm (right) in friendlier times.

Ernst Röhm was never the leader of the SA

The leader of the SA, of which there were five in all, was given the title of *Oberster SA-Führer* (Supreme SA Leader). Ernst Röhm never held this title. He was given the title of *Stabschef-SA* (Chief of Staff). This means that Röhm was never actually the supreme leader of the SA, 'merely' its sub-leader.

Röhm: Gay rights activist

The main justification given by Hitler for the Night of the Long Knives was that Ernst Röhm and the SA were planning a coup - the beginning of their 'second revolution'. Part of the anti-Röhm propaganda put out by Goebbels after the purge to persuade the general public that he was a dangerous and 'deviant' man, was the so called 'revelation' that he was a homosexual. Even for the general public, this was patently 'old news'. Not only was Hitler and other high-ranking Nazis well aware of Röhm's sexual orientation (he had never made a secret of it and had, in fact, argued in a number of circles for the decriminalisation of homosexuality in Germany), but the wider public had been made aware of it in 1925 and reminded of it in 1931. In 1925 Röhm endured a very public 'outing' when, after being robbed by one of his consorts, he chose to pursue the theft through the courts. By all accounts, he gave remarkably candid testimony, particularly given the times, about his homosexuality. In 1931 the Munich Post published private letters from Röhm to a friend of his which detailed his affairs with men as well as his desire to see homosexuality given the same legal protection as heterosexuality. Despite the NSDAP's stand in favour of Paragraph 175 of the German Penal Code - which outlawed homosexual acts - Röhm was never shy in decrying its provisions. The leader of the SA was a fervent advocate of a disciplined, powerful, warrior-like masculine homosexuality, the likes of which had, according to Röhm, been overpowered in the public imagination by the creeping femininity of a post war Europe dominated by a Bolshevism, a Judaism, and a bourgeoisie that all seemed to represent chaos and disorder. According to Eleanor Hancock, in her journal article, *"Only the Real, the True, the Masculine Held Its Value": Ernst Röhm, Masculinity, and Male Homosexuality,* Röhm was the very image of a "hyper-masculinity". He was powerful and scarred, and his demeanour was "...designed to counteract contemporary views of homosexuality as feminine". She goes on to stress that Röhm "...attached paramount importance to the values of militarized masculinity"[32]. By all accounts, despite his unconscionable right-wing thuggery and racist dogma, Ernst Röhm was rather progressive in the area of gay rights.

The Brownshirts: A name born of serendipity

The reason the SA wore brown uniforms, and therefore the reason for the name 'Brown Shirts', was because there was a superfluity of German uniforms left over from World War One. Great quantities had been ordered for troops posted to 'tropical' territories, particularly in North Africa, not long before the Armistice was signed on 11th November 1918. Once an end to hostilities was declared, the shirts became readily and, more importantly, cheaply available on the German market. Only later, once the NSDAP had sufficient funds, were the uniforms made to order. Thus, the name that can send shivers down the spine of democracies, was merely born of happenstance.

'Stormtroopers' and the Gymnastic and Sports Division

Although we associate the term 'stormtrooper' with the Nazi SA, it was commonly used throughout the latter stages of World War One as an informal name to describe German 'shock troops' (Stoßtruppen) whose role it was to infiltrate enemy trenches in smaller numbers, thus 'shocking' them with their speed and the element of surprise. If there is a lesson that George Lucas has taught us (other than to 'never go back'), it's that you don't have to be original to have an impact. The Nazis, ever a group with an eye to 'acquiring' symbolism and meaning from the past and using it to their advantage, employed the

---

[32] Hancock, E. *"Only the Real, the True, the Masculine Held Its Value": Ernst Röhm, Masculinity, and Male Homosexuality.* Journal of the History of Sexuality, Vol. 8, No. 4 (April 1998) pp. 616-641. University of Texas Press

moniker 'stormtrooper' in a similar way and for a similar purpose as they had employed the swastika, or the term führer: to encapsulate power and to instil fear. Having said this, if ever there was a name to have a less fearful impact on Nazi opponents than the one chosen by Hitler for an earlier incarnation of the SA in 1921, then this author struggled to find it. Before it became a formalised paramilitary for the Party and given its, now infamous, name, the Sturmabteilung was given a more euphemistic title when Hitler called it the *Gymnastic and Sports Division* (Turn- und Sportabteilun) *of the Party*. The reasoning behind the bizarre moniker was so as to deflect government curtailing of its violent activities. Nevertheless...

6

MEIN KAMPF, THE RESURRECTION BOOK: TWO VOLUMES AND A SEQUEL

WHAT YOU NEED TO KNOW

In the debris and chaos of a defeated Munich of 1945, an American officer who was sifting through documents of the Nazi Publishing house, commonly referred to as the *Eher-Verlag*, was handed a manuscript by the manager - Josef Berg - who had retrieved it from one of the safes in the building. The manuscript, along with hundreds of thousands, if not millions, of documents was confiscated by the Americans who had occupied Bavaria. The manuscript was then transferred to the United States whereupon it was housed in the US Army Archives in Washington D.C. There it sat until a young academic named Gerhard Weinberg, who was microfilming every document that had been confiscated in order that it be returned to Germany, came across it again. The year was 1958. As Weinberg went about his tedious business, he happened upon a box-file which he opened and explored, as he had done countless times before. However, this *green* box-file contained something very different to the usual bureaucratic tedium - the very 324 page manuscript that had been retrieved from the safe in the *Eher-Verlag*. Mislabelled, 'Draft of Mein Kampf', Weinberg had stumbled across something that had been rumoured to exist - hinted at in written recordings and discussed only tangentially in National Socialist circles: the sequel to *Mein Kampf*.

WHY IT'S IMPORTANT THAT YOU KNOW THIS

After the embarrassing failure of the Munich Putsch[33], Hitler was found guilty of treason and sentenced to five years in Landsberg Prison - a relatively small but certainly comfortable penal confinement located in the South West of Bavaria, about 40 miles from Munich. Taking much of a 'wing' on the second floor of the prison which, according to prison documents (see website below), was referred to as *Feldherrenhügel,* or 'General's Hill', the inmate who arrived on April Fool's Day of 1924, wanted for very little. Hitler received a great many visitors, one of whom - Ernst Hanfstaengl - was an intimate friend of Adolf Hitler. Speaking of one of his many visits, Hanfstaengl commented that he felt as if he had "...walked into a delicatessen. There was fruit and there were flowers, wine and other alcoholic beverages, ham, sausage, cake, boxes of chocolates and much more"[34].

Hitler would spend only 294 days behind bars but during his comfortable incarceration in Landsberg, Hitler either typed or dictated (to Rudolf Hess - one of his prison mates) what would go on to be published as *Mein Kampf,* or *My Struggle.*

Initially, Mein Kampf was something of a novelty success - selling all 10,000 copies of its first print run - after all, this was

---

[33] The Munich Putsch of 1923 was an attempt by Hitler and the Nazis to take control of the Bavarian government, hoping to spark a nationwide uprising against the Weimar government of Germany. The resounding failure of this coup should have resulted in either a long sentence or execution for treason. Neither of these things happened, in part because of the sympathy he enjoyed in the courtroom – particularly from the judge.

[34] Friedmann, J. (2010) *Flowers for the Führer in Landsberg Prison.* Available at: http://www.spiegel.de/international/germany/adolf-hitler-s-time-in-jail-flowers-for-the-fuehrer-in-landsberg-prison-a-702159.html (Accessed: June 2018)

---

written by the little corporal that had tried to take over Bavaria. Hitler was desperate for his tome to be a success, for he had amassed a considerable debt due to legal fees and court costs. However, the book, very much like Hitler himself during the second half of the 1920's, remained little more than a novelty, and sales of the second print run collapsed. In spite of a second volume of *Mein Kampf* being published in 1926, sales were desperately slow. The book suffered from a number of environmental developments that hindered its popularity. After the chaos of the early Weimar years of 1918-1923, which saw attempted revolutions, putsches (including Hitler's own), invasions, and economic collapse, the period immediately following was relatively stable and prosperous. During these 'Stresemann Years', the 'Golden Years', or however it has since been described by posterity, German people, on the whole, weren't suffering in the same way they had been once World War One designated them as the losers. As a clear result of this less desperate environment, the average German was not particularly interested in the extremist politics espoused by parties such as the Nazis, or by their mouthpieces - no matter how magnetic they may have been.

Much of Mein Kampf, Volume I is devoted to the early, formative and, frankly, miserable life of its author. It broadly and obviously attempts to paint his life as one ordained by history's brush - an unfortunate child, put-upon by the external and controlling forces of a darkly malicious and, crucially, anti-German, conspiracy, who would ultimately triumph. In this narrative, Hitler embodied the trials of the German people against their own 'dark conspiracy' - that of international Jewry and Bolshevism. Learning from their twinned pasts, Hitler and the German peoples would rise, in a feat of predestined will to power - like a double-headed phoenix rising from the ashes of World War One - and restore *themselves* to their rightful places in history. As a result, Mein Kampf became a way to identify the problems of the past as well as a path to follow. In this turgid, poorly written rehash of debunked racial 'science' and glorified self-reference, the future of Germany was to be found. Unfortunately, in a post Munich Putsch Germany, there seemed to be little need for Adolf Hitler, and even less for his book, whether it be Volume I *or* Volume II. As the 1920's were drawing to an end, Hitler and his ideas were very close to being irrelevant - a designation that is terminal to any political party with their eyes on power.

In an attempt to arrest this decline in political relevance - something hammered home by the terrible showing of the National Socialists in the 1928 elections (they won only 12 seats in the Reichstag out of a possible 491) - as well as the dwindling sales of *Mein Kampf* (which had all but ceased, after the novelty of it had worn off), Hitler began writing another book. It was this 324-page work that was discovered by Gerhard Weinberg in 1958. This was to signal Hitler's regeneration in political life, recalibrate his views on everything from foreign policy (suggesting an alliance with England) to military power, and to reassert the common tropes of earlier (race, lebensraum, and war). According to available evidence, only two copies of the manuscript were ever made. One of them sat on the lap of an unbelieving Gerhard Weinberg in 1958; the other has never been found. Unfortunately for Hitler, this new manuscript became a victim of the environment which had persuaded him to write it in the first place. His publisher, the *Eher Verlag*, convinced Hitler that any new publication by him would merely cannibalise the already meagre sales of the two volumes of Mein Kampf that were still struggling to find an audience in the relative prosperity of Stresemann's Germany. Consequently, the manuscript remained under wraps and largely forgotten except for the occasional passing mention by Hitler himself - only one of which was recorded in 1942 (in Hitler's 'Table Talk'; discussed later in this chapter). Hitler would be long dead before his *Zweites Buch* would be resurrected and published. A resurrection in the fortunes of *Mein Kampf* would not be so long in coming.

As counterfactual as the following may seem (and of course it is), both volumes of *Mein Kampf,* as well as the *Zweites Buch,* would most likely have served little historical purpose other than that of curiosities, had the *environment* - both world and German - not shifted in favour of the National Socialists. Perhaps a clear argument for the structuralists emerges from the environmental prerequisite of the Wall Street Crash and ensuing Great Depression for the re-emergence of Hitler and the NSDAP on the national scene after 1929 - a year unlike any other in the interwar period. As Germans began to turn their attention to solutions to the economic and social hardships as offered by extremist parties, Mein Kampf became an entirely different animal - one which grew teeth.

Picture 36: Hitler's Second Book, published long after the death of its author

In many ways, *Mein Kampf* (Volumes I and II) would come to reflect the changing fortunes of the Nazis pre-1945, whereas the muted public reception to the *Zweites Buch* could be said to reflect the understandable post-war reluctance by many Germans to come to terms with what had happened in their country. Mein Kampf, very much like Hitler, would experience a resurrection in the period following the Wall Street Crash - a resurrection that would see it become a broad ideological focus for the Party members, a guide for those looking to understand the political *nature* of National Socialist goals, as well as a biographical retelling of the (dramatic, often fictional and largely functional) genesis of Hitler's belief in his own 'destiny'. Perhaps more importantly, in so far as the horrors that would ultimately be carried out either in his name, his image, or on his orders, Mein Kampf (Volumes I and II) detailed Hitler's racial beliefs. The publication, as it had always done, offered convenient scapegoats and a simple manifesto for action, but now it had an added urgency created, in part, by the associated problems of the Great Depression and, in part, by the Party's relentless pushing of their agenda and the book. Perhaps an argument for a mixture of structuralism and intentionalism. After 1929, *Mein Kampf* became one of the Nazi Party's most reliable, effective, as well as profitable, methods of propaganda. Hitler became a millionaire in the process and Mein Kampf, during the years 1929-33, found itself well on the way to a ubiquity that would help lay the foundation for one of the few ideological constants of the Nazi regime after 1933: anti-Semitism. Throughout both volumes, the demonising and denigration of the world's Jews is relentless; in Chapter XI, entitled *Race and People*, Hitler takes almost every page to 'prove' the superiority of the Aryan race while simultaneously 'determining' the inadequacy of the Jewish one. The very first chapter of Volume II, entitled *Weltanschauung and Party*, contains some of Hitler's more paranoid anti-Semitism, the type of which would ultimately lead him to his well-known and appalling conclusions:

"At a blow they would awaken the bourgeois world to see the madness of thinking that the Jewish drive towards world-conquest can be effectually opposed by means of Western Democracy." (MK, Vol II, p.293).

In the *Zweites Buch,* Hitler spends the first chapter discussing his version of natural selection and the general role of war and struggle in the process of racial development; it takes him until Chapter 2 before he gets specific:

"Above all, they are breeding grounds of blood mixing and bastardisation, and of race lowering, thus resulting in those purulent infection centres in which the international Jewish racial maggots thrive and finally effect further destruction."[35]

The following chapter, *Race and Will in the Struggle for Power,* unpacks his racial ideas even further.

When the Zweites Buch was first published in 1961, fully entitled *Hitler's Zweites Buch: Ein Dokument Aus Dem Jahr 1928*, it was edited by Gerhard Weinberg and published by the Munich Institute. Both publisher and editor refused payment. Perhaps weary of the Nazi years, the *Zweites Buch*, failed to find an audience beyond academia. To this day, finding someone that has even heard of Hitler's sequel to Mein Kampf, let alone read it, is a rare challenge indeed. However, even the briefest examination of the sale and publication data of Hitler's works (in concert with other indicators) would go a long way in helping to gauge the 'relevance' of National Socialism in any given year between the years 1925-45 (although from 1939 onwards, the issue becomes infinitely more complicated because of the war). If you are looking for a barometer of the post-war movement towards reconciliation, perhaps the attention (or lack thereof) garnered by the *Zweites Buch* could

---

[35] Hitler, A. (1928) *Hitler's Zweites Buch Ein Dokument Aus Dem Jahr 1928.* Chapter II. p. 14. Herausgegeben vom Institut für Zeitgeschichte

equally serve a purpose. As such, these books very much go through cycles of resurrection...

WHAT THIS IS CONNECTED TO

Volksgemeinschaft/the People's Community

We know Hitler believed that the traditional 'success' of the Prussian state was cultivated, in substantial part, by the supposed cloistered purity of its peoples. In order for his vision of the Third Reich to be realised - for the destiny of the Prussian people to be fulfilled - Hitler was convinced that there must be a purification of the bloodlines. He went so far as to suggest that, *"In standing guard against the Jew I am defending the handiwork of the Lord"* (MK, Vol I, p.61). The creation of a 'pure' German community - a *Volksgemeinschaft* - would form the foundation of the *Thousand Year Reich*. The prescription for doing so would be found in *Mein Kampf:* get rid of the Jews.

Propaganda and profit

As with all totalitarian regimes, by definition, the state must control *every* aspect of *everyone's* lives. Consequently, Mein Kampf was also a tool of *gleichschaltung* or *coordination*. *Coordination* was the euphemism used by Hitler as a substitute for the word 'control'. Consequently, the book served twin purposes: a far-reaching and intimate ideological indoctrination, and an individual proof of loyalty. The former drove the *coordination* of thought, the latter drove the *coordination* of action.

It should come as no surprise that, since there are two chapters within the two volumes of Mein Kampf devoted to the issue of propaganda (and the *Zweites Buch* is dense with discussion of it), the book itself would be used as a core element of indoctrination and persuasion of the German people. There were clear attempts by Goebbels to embed the book within the administrative and ideological superstructure of Nazi Germany. It is without doubt that they were largely successful in doing this. Even without the efforts of the propaganda machinery of the Third Reich, the publisher of Mein Kampf during the 'Hitler Years' - the *Eher Verlag* - exploited Hitler's popularity and began ferociously marketing the book. This strategy resurrected the book from near-death, succeeding, in terms of copies sold, beyond the predictions of anyone at the publishing house.

As a means of driving sales, the *Eher Verlag* began repackaging Mein Kampf in an attempt to target specific audiences and exploit particular events. For example, there were commemorative editions such as the one produced for Hitler's 50th birthday, every newly married couple received a copy of the 'Marriage Edition', and there were braille editions for the blind. Most ceremonies of one form or another involved the giving and receiving of Mein Kampf. Having said this, (and this is crucial), very few were 'given away' - although they might have been free in some cases to the recipient, they were always purchased somewhere along the route from publisher to consumer. This meant, of course, that Hitler became very wealthy - which was just as well because, prior to him being sworn in as Chancellor, he owed significant sums to banks and the 'tax man' (although this debt was conveniently wiped out when he became Chancellor). The book became a staple in the homes of any German who wanted to show their faith in the Führer and the Nazis, look for guidance in National Socialist ideology, or out of fear of being labelled an 'opponent'.

By the end of World War Two, Mein Kampf had sold around 12 million copies. The question that clearly needs to be asked, however, is this: how many of these books were actually read? Of course, this is an impossible question to answer. Nonetheless, it is an important question to digest, particularly when attempting to determine the impact and influence of the book on the people of Germany.

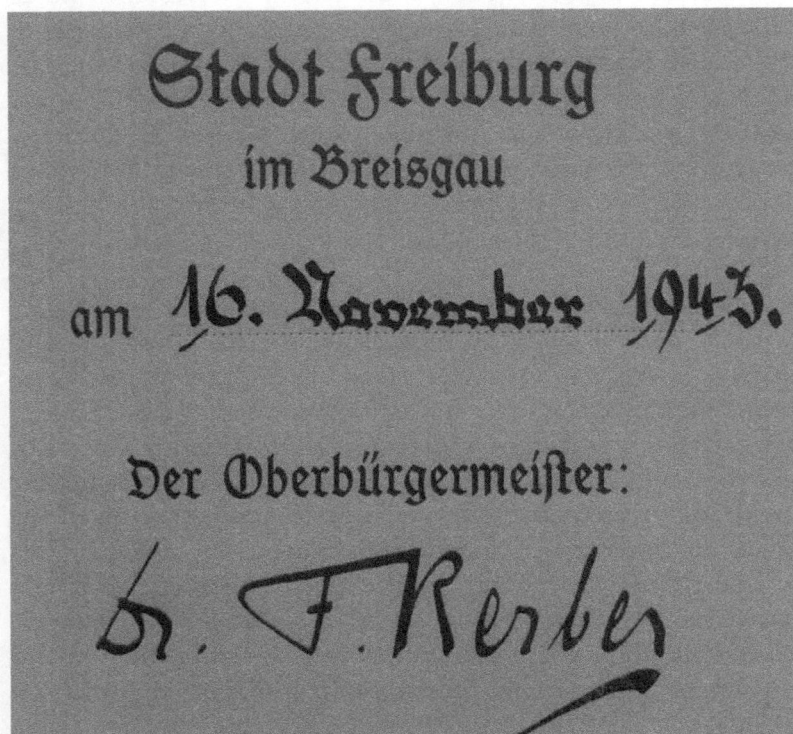

Picture 37: Signature of Franz Kerber, mayor of Freiburg im Breisgau, 1943. Standard frontpage dedication of Mein Kampf to newlyweds.

Bible or Little Red Book?

Hitler saw his party not simply as a political movement, but also a social, cultural and religious (or 'spiritual') one. In Mein Kampf, Hitler wrote the following: *"I believe today that my conduct is in accordance with the will of the Almighty Creator"* (MK, Vol I, p. 61). There are conflicting views about Hitler's religiosity, but most historians tend to agree that any professing of support for Christianity in Germany was merely a tool of political expediency - useful conciliations to the millions of Protestants and Catholics in Germany, and a necessary deference to the institutional might of their respective churches. That is until he and the Nazis were in a position of preeminent power across Europe, at which point he would erase it and replace it. With Nazism. Regardless, Mein Kampf was used by the National Socialists as a none-too-subtle substitute for the Bible. From the literal replacing of the Bible with Mein Kampf as the central text for *Positive Christianity*, which helped drive the German Faith Movement and the Reich Church, to the reciting of text from the book in schools instead of the Bible. In a similar fashion to Mao's 'Little Red Book', Mein Kampf was not only the 'revealed truth' of the Party, it also claimed proof that the *Leader* was somehow fulfilling a 'messiah-like' destiny. Both the Little Red Book and Mein Kampf helped foster and then synthesise the cults of Mao and Hitler. Both leaders became an intrinsic and inseparable part of their own 'Holy Trinities': The Father (the state), the Son (Mao/Hitler), and the Holy Ghost (China and Germany's glorified histories, to be *resurrected* in the future).

Despite the largely failed Nazi attempts to coordinate the Christian Churches of Germany, Mein Kampf *was* successful in presenting Hitler's ideas and it was *used* successfully as a staple of Nazi propaganda, presenting the 'glory' and 'omniscience' of Hitler using a thoroughly integrated methodology. Having said this, however, the question still remains: *how many people actually read it?* Naturally, evidence that it was ever read by the newly married couples, or listened to by the congregations, or taken from the bookshelves of average Germans, is mostly anecdotal. Consequently, the true impact of Mein Kampf, in the everyday lives of Germans under the Nazi regime can never be fully calibrated. Some have tried. A number may even have succeeded, to a degree. In his leviathan of investigation and research - *Adolf Hitler's "Mein Kampf", 1922-1945* - Othmar Plöckinger subverts the common notion that the book remained an unread bestseller: "You just need to look at the high frequency with which it was borrowed from the library to be able to say that it certainly didn't gather dust on the shelf,"[36]

Lebensraum

One of the core narrative threads, woven none-too-subtly through Mein Kampf, is Hitler's belief that the German state was overcrowded and its people - the pure, racially superior, *Herrenvolk* - needed 'living space'. In the chapter entitled, *Eastern Orientation or Eastern Policy* (Chapter XIV, Vol II), Hitler built upon half a century of spurious racialist theory and German imperialist ambition, to reassert the peculiarly German myth of a predestined and pre-eminent empire that would stretch across Europe. Particularly Eastern Europe. Lebensraum, or *living space* - the belief that the superior Aryan race should conquer land to the east and use it for the resettlement of a too-densely populated German people - was a familiar trope peddled by nationalists of the previous fifty years. Hitler, as ever, was entirely unoriginal. Unfortunately, when Hitler became *Führer* and Mein Kampf became a source of gospel and doctrine for Nazi supporters, the myth became a terrible reality and the natural conclusion to eastern expansion was the annihilation of those deemed racially unfit to occupy the land that had been reserved for the *Herrenvolk*. The message of *Lebensraum*, as with much of what appeared in Mein Kampf, was reinforced by repetition and, by virtue of the numbers of books sold and foisted upon people by Josef Goebbels, became popular, actionable, and righteous. Although unpublished under the Third Reich, the *Zweites Buch*, goes to great efforts to explain and justify Hitler's desire for living space; an entire chapter, *German Needs and Aims*, revolves around this core concern:

[36] Plöckinger, O. (2016) Adolf Hitler's "Mein Kampf", 1922-1945. Germany. De Gruyter Oldenbourg

"For the sense of a sound territorial policy lies in the fact that a Folk's living space is enlarged by allotting new areas for settlement to the surplus of the population which, then, if it is not to take on the character of an emigration, must be in close political and governmental relation with the mother country."[37]

WHAT YOU DIDN'T KNOW WILL BLOW YOUR MIND

'Hitler's *Table Talk*' and that 'one mention'

It probably comes as little surprise that Hitler liked to hear the sound of his own voice, often holding court and extemporising from one subject to the next, with little to no regard for coherence. Apparently for Martin Bormann, Hitler's private secretary, it was not enough that only the Führer's immediate power-circle ever got to receive those words. Bormann suggested to Hitler that his private conversations (or, rather, his monologues) be recorded for posterity, so that his intimate theorising could be appreciated in future years. Bormann, Heinrich Heim, and Henry Picker were all selected for the prestigious responsibility of taking notes in shorthand of the Führer's words. After the war, these notes were variously (and separately) published by the 'note-takers', who quarrelled about publishing rights. The first to publish was Henry Picker, who did so in 1951. The book was titled, *Hitler's Tischgespräche im Führerhauptquartier*, or *Hitler's Table Talks at Führer Headquarters*. It is in one of these 'table talks' that the existence of the *Zweites Buch* is confirmed. There is one mention and only one mention.

---

[37] [37] Hitler, A. (1928) *Hitler's Zweites Buch Ein Dokument Aus Dem Jahr 1928.* Chapter VI. p. 41. Herausgegeben vom Institut für Zeitgeschichte

Mein Kampf's original title

Originally, Mein Kampf was to be titled *Four and a Half Years of Struggle Against Lies, Stupidity and Cowardice*, but Hitler's publisher convinced him that, bearing in mind his current standing as a treasonous outcast, a less inflammatory title might be more...marketable.

Dedication

One of comedian Dennis Miller's early jokes was that it was possible to judge how much of an 'asshole Hitler was' by the fact that he did not dedicate *Mein Kampf* to anyone - thus demonstrating, tongue firmly in cheek, his heartlessness. On the contrary, except for the heartlessness, Miller was way off. Hitler's 1925 book did indeed have a dedication - to the sixteen fallen 'heroes' who died during the failed Munich Putsch. In an early example of Hitler mixing history, ideology, and propaganda, this dedication was melodramatic and bold, bearing in mind he was in prison for treason when he wrote it.

Hitler drove a Mercedes but was *driven* by Henry Ford

Henry Ford, the American pioneer of the mass-produced motorcar, was held in high esteem by Adolf Hitler, primarily because of his very public hatred of Jews. Aside from his motorcar company, Ford also owned a number of publishing concerns. One of these was *The Dearborn Independent*. To all intents and purposes, the *Dearborn* was the personal mouthpiece of the industrial magnate. And he was a rabid anti-Semite. In the very early 1920s, the weekly newspaper ran stories detailing evidence of the 'evil of Jewry', and many of these stories were later bound into a risible four volume series called, *The*

International Jew: The World's Foremost Problem[38]. The success of Henry Ford in industry was admired by early National Socialists - particularly during the early, turbulent, years of the Weimar Republic. The public anti-Semitism of one of America's greatest industrialists was also admired. Adolf Hitler mentions only one American in the first edition of Mein Kampf - a reverential reference to Henry Ford in conjunction with his ability to triumph despite the 'control' of American Jews. It seems that it is clearly more than an anecdote that Hitler displayed a photograph of Henry Ford above his desk.

Land of the Aryans: Why Persia changed its name to Iran

According to Dilip Hiro, in his book, *Iran Under the Ayatollahs*, the Shah of Persia was persuaded by the Iranian Ambassador to Germany, as an act of "Aryan solidarity" with Nazi Germany, to change his country's name to Iran in 1935[39]. In fact, many Persians who occupied the upper echelons of their society, identified themselves as Aryans and wholeheartedly supported Nazi ideology - as they were persuaded to understand it. The name Iran, used well before the first century BC, means '*The Land of Aryans*'.

One final resurrection?

While the original version of Mein Kampf remains prohibited in Germany, an academic reprinting with an extra 1300 pages of notes drawing keen attention the half-truths, misrepresentations, and outright lies told by Hitler, was published in January 2016 by the German Institute of

---

[38] Ford, H. (1920-1922) *The International Jew: The World's Foremost Problem.* Abridged version published by Martino Fine Books (2011)
[39] Hiro, Dilip. (2013) *Iran Under the Ayatollahs.* UK. Routledge & Kegan Paul Inc., p.296

Contemporary History. Designed to satisfy curiosity and diminish the 'mystique' of Mein Kampf, the original print run of 4,000 copies was woefully inadequate. The book became a bestseller in Germany, but this time in 2016. It is also, curiously, very popular in other countries, such as India, Bangladesh, and Turkey (though it is currently banned there).

THE HITLER PRINCIPLE: TURNING A FAMILIAR GERMAN NOUN INTO A BYWORD FOR TYRANNY

WHAT YOU NEED TO KNOW

Ricardo Klement, a resident of Buenos Aires, Argentina, was bundled into the back of a car on the way back from work on 11 May 1960. Klement's son, Klaus, had been dating a young lady named Sophie Hermann, the daughter of Lothar, a man who had emigrated from Germany in 1938. Ricardo Klement was injected with a heavy sedative and, with his unconscious head in the lap of Rafi Eitan, who was sitting in the backseat of the car, he was removed to a safe house. After interrogation, Ricardo Klement was taken from the safe house and transported, still barely conscious, on an El Al plane out of Argentina. El Al Airlines is the national carrier for Israel. Rafi Eitan was one of the dozen or so Israeli Mossad agents tasked with the abduction and removal of Ricardo Klement from Argentina to Israel in, what was codenamed, *Operation Finale*. It was Hermann Lothar, the daughter of whom was dating Klaus, that had alerted Mossad to Klaus' father Ricardo Klement. In the next two years, Ricardo Klement would become, perhaps, the most infamous man on the planet. For Ricardo Klement was, in fact, Adolf Eichmann - SS *Obersturmbannführer* and the Nazi architect of the Final Solution.

After Germany's defeat in the war, Eichmann managed, with the help of elements within the Catholic Church, to escape through the 'ratline'[40] to Argentina, whereupon he lived until 1960. He was tracked down and abducted by Mossad, who took him to Israel to stand trial for his crimes.

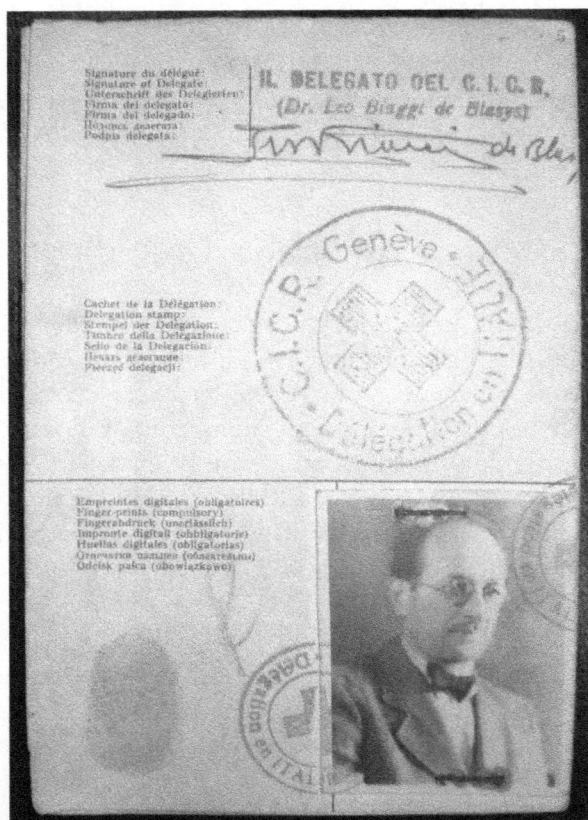

Picture 38: Red Cross identity document used by Eichmann to enter Argentina as Ricardo Klement

---

[40] 'Ratlines' was a term used to describe the networks of escape across Europe that were employed by senior Nazis after World War Two. The 'ratlines' would take fleeing Nazis to safe havens – often in Latin America. For a phenomenal investigation of these, listen to the BBC's *The Ratline* podcast series. It can be found here:
https://www.bbc.co.uk/programmes/p04sj2pt

Given the nature of Nazi atrocities, Eichmann's trial was naturally going to be controversial. Immediately following Israel's announcement that it had kidnapped and smuggled Eichmann out of Argentina with the express intention of trying him in the newly-created country, international discussions, arbitrations, and arguments began. An unprecedented conundrum had arranged itself for the international legal system: can a person who committed a crime in one country but is resident in another be tried by a country that didn't even exist when the crime was committed? As if this wasn't challenging enough of a set of circumstances, Eichmann used as his principle line of defence the argument that would become a notorious and now commonly used exculpation for those that have engaged in state organised terror; an argument that attempts to enable the perpetrator to distance themselves from their actions, thus removing their responsibility for them: that of *simply following orders*. Eichmann's defence was unprecedented because it was underpinned by his invocation of an organisational and leadership principle that was entirely unique to Nazi Germany: ***the führerprinzip.***

WHY IT'S IMPORTANT THAT YOU KNOW THIS

Literally translated from German, the führerprinzip means 'leader principle'. Although we, as modern historians, tend to associate the term 'führer' or, more specifically, '*the* Führer', with Hitler and his authority, it was a term that would have been very familiar to Germans *well before* his arrival on the political scene.

The *führerprinzip* would have been particularly familiar to those German men with experience in the armed forces because it denoted a man whose superior experience was to be respected. The term was a very common ascription given to anyone who led, or who held superior experience. Although the term has died out in German political usage (for obvious reasons), it still very much remains common in compound words. For example, if you happened to be a *Tourist Guide* in Germany today, you would be called a *Fremden-führer.*

In German party politics (pre-Hitler), the führerprinzip was simply an organizational principle - someone was the leader of the party and they should be respected as such. Theresa May is the current Prime Minister of Great Britain and the leader of the Conservative Party (at the time of writing); in Germany of the 1920's, she would have been called *Conservative Party Führer.* Nothing in the least unusual. Hitler forced the NSDAP to accept him as their undisputed führer in 1921 when there was the threat of merging with another right-wing party. He would then expand its meaning to include an entire nation when, in 1934, President Hindenburg died and he conjoined the offices of Chancellor and President to become '*the* Führer'. Later, in 1941 (when the war was going well for the Nazis), Hitler rebranded himself as '*Germanic* Führer' - the leader of all Northern German-Nordic Europeans.

Hitler forced a mutation of the term *führerprinzip*, and this is the root of its importance to, what would become, Nazi Germany. It would also be central to the legal defences offered by Nazis at the Nuremberg Trials and Adolf Eichmann's in Israel. Hitler and Joseph Goebbels understood the ideological and political meaning that could be drawn/unpacked from the word, *führer,* and added a 'religious/spiritual/cultish' dimension. In a speech given by Rudolf Hess in 1934, he invokes divinity by saying that Hitler "...is the instrument of the will of a higher power...because he is a true Führer"[41]. They then used it to convince many German people, within and without the party, that Hitler was deserving of a higher, God-like, status - one that

---

[41] *Hess, R.* From a speech given in 1938 entitled, *Die Wahl Adolf Hitlers zum Führer.* The speech was taken from the, *Reden.* Munich. Zentralverlag der NSDAP. pp. 52-63

demanded a redoubtable loyalty, unquestioning obedience and offered, in return, an omniscient rectitude of action. Buried in the word, *führer*, and the term *führerprinzip* (in the way the Nazis used them both) was so much subtlety of meaning that many Germans could not help but be impressed by Hitler (Note: being impressed does not necessarily imply a positive connotation). In the middle of the dramatic and tragic uncertainty of the Great Depression, Hitler represented an appealing dual symbolism to the people of Germany that was both reminiscent of the powerful German past of the Kaiserreich and foretelling of a new *Reich*. A *Thousand Year Reich*. Once *in* power, this new deviation in an old noun's meaning, is what helped the Nazi State convince hundreds of thousands of ordinary Germans to, not only accept some of the horrors it wrought, but also to carry those horrors out willingly.

WHAT THIS IS CONNECTED TO

The führerprinzip is born in Bamberg

After the Munich Putsch of 1923, during which the Nazis failed to take power in the German state of Bavaria, Hitler was imprisoned in Landsberg whereupon he took the time to write his risible magnum opus - *Mein Kampf*. Whilst imprisoned, the National Socialists were banned (in November 1923) and total party collapse looked imminent. Although the Party continued in a different guise - as the *German Party* - infighting and regional differences regarding direction, looked set to relegate both Hitler and the Party to a mere footnote in world history. That is, until Hitler reasserted control at the Bamberg Conference in 1926.

Bamberg, in northern Bavaria, was chosen by Hitler as the location for an all-Party conference in 1926 (discussed earlier in this book) that would settle any and all issues related to division and direction. The selection of Bavaria was symbolic - it clearly represented to Nazi Party members where Hitler believed the centre of the Party to be - in the south. A clear schism had developed within the Nazi Party, between those in the north - seen as urban and socialist - and those in the south - seen as provincial and racialist. Gregor Strasser and Joseph Goebbels represented the north while Hitler and Gottfried Feder, the south.

Why is this relevant? It was at this meeting that Hitler, with a two hour speech, united the Party, sidelined all political opponents, fixed the ideological and political direction of the National Socialists, and solidified his position as their undisputed leader. He did much of this by invoking the *führerprinzip*. From this point onwards, Adolf Hitler was not simply the NSDAP führer, he was *The Führer*.

'Working towards the führer' and the death of Hindenburg

Hitler became Chancellor of Germany in January 1933 but both he *and* the National Socialists were in positions of relative weakness. Ultimately, that weakness manifested itself in the figure of President Hindenburg who held a position framed, in all ways by the Weimar Constitution, as the Chancellor's superior. At any point, President Hindenburg could remove Hitler as Chancellor and call another election. He could also rule (as set down in *Article 48* of the Constitution) by 'decree'. This meant that, should Hindenburg decide to declare an 'emergency', his power would be absolute. As long as the Weimar Constitution and the much-loved Paul von Hindenburg existed, Hitler would never be Germany's führer, much less *Germanic Führer*.

When President Hindenburg died on the morning of the 2nd of August 1934, Hitler acted with a swiftness that spoke of a clear purpose and design. A law, cynically backdated to the 1st of

August, was announced by the Reich Government which ordained that, in the event of the death of Hindenburg, the office of the Reich President was to be combined with that of the Reich Chancellor. The law specifically, and unusually, named Adolf Hitler as the recipient of these newly combined positions. It also specifically referred to Hitler as *'the Führer'*. Hitler was no longer a mere politician, or even a holder of the highest office in the land. He was *the Führer*.

Much academic energy has been expended trying to determine the true nature of Hitler's rule over Germany, the majority of which has centred around the debate between intentionalist and structuralist interpretations. Essentially, the question most frequently asked is this: Was Hitler a decisive dictator, at the centre of every important decision, or was he a weak and lazy dictator, responding mainly to events as they occurred, and allowing those around him to determine policy and outcome? There is clear evidence to support both of these interpretations, if you wish to seek it out. There is, however, a third option. An option put forward by Ian Kershaw[42]: that of *working towards the Führer*.

In the way that Kershaw meant it (if I dare be so bold as to presume) was that the nature of Hitler's rule fell somewhere between the two interpretations. He was most certainly uninterested in the daily administration of government. He rose late and slept late. Other than in issues of the military and race, Hitler was less than proactive. However, those areas in which he took an interest, Hitler directed with a fanatical (in the case of the military during World War Two - mostly incompetent) zeal. Somewhere between these two extremes, Kershaw found a middle ground: He was both lazy and zealous, in equal but inconstant measure. But he was *always* the *führer*. Surely, this is a

---

[42] Kershaw, Ian (2001) *The "Hitler Myth": Image and Reality in the Third Reich.* Oxford University Press.

paradox - can there *be* such a thing as a lazy or inconstant *führer*? Well, according to Kershaw, there can.

'Working towards the führer' is a remarkably fluid model of leadership and governance but it does seem to explain the functioning of Nazi Germany. Supported by Max Weber's 'Charismatic theory of leadership', Kershaw's thesis goes something like this: Hitler was always central in the mind of those who determined and carried out Nazi policy, but he could hardly be ascribed the ability, intelligence, or even the drive to plan, organise, and shape, the detail and nature of policies which would move 68 million Germans to action across a 12 year period. People within Germany, both those who directly carried out National Socialist policies or were complicit in affording them the room to germinate and grow to near unstoppable forces, did so by *interpreting* the *Führer's* wishes.

According to Kershaw, it's simple logistics: no one man, let alone someone as inconstant in his energies as Hitler, could possibly determine the structural mechanics of national policy, never mind the organisational minutiae of these policies. Individuals - thousands, if not millions of them - did this, and they did it in a way *they* thought accorded best with the *Führer's* wishes, whatever *they* were. As a result, Nazi Germany seemed to be organised and run by deputy, sub, and assistant *führers*, the majority of whom simply did what they *thought* they should do. This was Kershaw's interpretation of the führerprinzip as it applied to Germany after January 1933. The importance of this interpretation should not be understated, either then *or* today - it recognises the wildly varying practices of regional Nazi Gauleiters and it ensures that blame for some of the more horrific dimensions of Nazi Germany be shared amongst those beyond Adolf Hitler, while never ignoring his importance at the centre of them. If we accept *working towards the führer* as reality, then it provides valuable *grey areas* within which fellow Nazis could root their arguments and justifications for actions undertaken in the name of Adolf Hitler. It was in these *grey areas* that Adolf Eichmann, recently of Argentina, attempted to anchor his testimony when on trial in Israel.

Picture 39: Adolf Eichmann invokes the führerprinzip while on trial in Israel

The death of democracy and the birth of the German Führer: if Hitler wills it then it is legal

On August 2nd, 1934, President Paul von Hindenburg died of lung cancer at the age of 86. Seeing the end coming, Hitler rushed a law through the Reichstag the day before his death. The *Law Concerning the Highest State Office of the Reich*, was a proactive and cynical piece of legislation that stipulated in the event of the death of the president, all powers residing in that office would automatically pass to the chancellor. The office of Reich Chancellor, as well as that cf Reich President, were effectively buried alongside the old General. The moment Hindenburg took his final breath, Hitler became, ostensibly, the 'Führer of the German Volk'. He was at once elevated above the Party by becoming the living embodiment of National Socialism; he was able to position himself *beyond* the law, because he had destroyed the Weimar Constitution. Politics ceased to exist, for what need is there for such a thing when Hitler, as *The Führer*, is the 'voice of Germany'? The *führerprinzip* had personalised the Party, the ideology, the country, the legal system, as well as the solutions to all of Germany's problems. Perhaps never before in history has so much of the anatomy of a state been conflated so successfully and so rapidly into the sole possession of one man. From this point onwards, whatever Hitler wills, it will be so.

The Volksgemeinschaft and the 'Final Solution'

Adolf Hitler would often blame Germany's loss in World War One, as well as her subsequent sufferings during the Weimar years, on the disintegration and dilution of the 'racial purity' of the Volksgemeinschaft, or 'Peoples Community'. According to Hitler and the National Socialists, racial weaknesses within the German 'People's Community', through interbreeding with racially impure 'non-Germans', had led to a degrading of the traditional strength of Germany. The German Volksgenosse, or 'National Comrades', who made up the 'People's Community', had fallen victim to negative eugenics, or poor breeding. As a result, Germany had become a weak victim-state instead of the powerful dominant-state it had always been.

Hitler's solution to this 'problem' was simple: create a stronger country by breeding a 'purer' people. The return of a purer German Volksgenosse would see the return of a stronger German Volksgemeinschaft, which would, in turn, serve as the foundation upon which the Nazis would build their *Thousand Year Reich*. Hitler would spend his years out of power cultivating and disseminating these ideas within the Party; he would spend his years *in* power attempting to put these ideas into practice across Germany. Or rather, *other people* would put these ideas into practice.

Of course, such spurious, not to mention mostly illegal, notions of racialism would be very difficult to carry out across Germany and then Europe. Hitler wasn't going to do it. Thus, it was left to his subordinates to interpret the *führer's* wishes. By 'working towards the führer', the creation of a new Volksgemeinschaft was left largely in the hands of others. They knew *roughly* what Hitler desired; they decided *roughly* how to achieve those desires. In many cases, individuals within the Party looking to advance their positions would find that a zealous approach to pursuing what they thought were Hitler's wishes, often brought praise from the führer, regardless of the means by which they achieved their outcomes. Hence, as Kershaw sees it, the ad hoc and uneven, yet horrifyingly extreme, way the racist policies of the Nazis were organised and executed - up to and including the 'Final Solution' - were a direct product of those competing within the structure forged out of the *führerprinzip*.

WHAT YOU DIDN'T KNOW WILL BLOW YOUR MIND

The Hitler salute: from Rome to Roosevelt

Bound up in the cultish worship of the *führer* and the creation of the *führerprinzip*, are the salutes and greetings of the National Socialists. Anyone with even a passing knowledge of Nazi Germany, will recognise *"Heil Hitler"*, *"Seig Heil"*, and *"Heil mein Führer"* as expressions embedded within the terrible theatre of National Socialism. These greetings and exclamations were no mere accident of gesture-evolution. Despite the words 'seig' and 'heil' having served as greetings within Germany long before the Nazi Party adopted them, they quickly became elemental requisites of the *führerprinzip*. Used, where appropriate, with the Nazi salute - raising and extending the right arm and hand to neck height - the language and symbolism of a *"Heil Hitler"* greeting was as much a piece of socially galvanising propaganda, a tool of obedience, a demonstration of loyalty to the *führer*, and an embodiment of a belief in Hitler's ideology, as it was a greeting.

Putting the spoken element of the greeting to one side, it is a matter of high interest and debate as to the origin of the salute itself - often termed, derogatorily, by many Germans at the time of its introduction into the political landscape by the National Socialists, as the *Roman salute*. Although it has been asserted that the salute has its origins in ancient Rome, there is scant proof of this other than eighteenth century art depicting it in a Roman setting. The reason for its initial, limited, acceptance from ordinary Germans as well as some NSDAP members, was that it was seen as a mere copy of the salute of Mussolini's Fascist Party - and this meant it was *unGermanic*. Regardless, in 1926 the Party made the greeting - salute and 'Heil Hitler'- compulsory. From this point onwards, the greeting became inseparable from the party and Hitler. It would later be further embedded into the fabric of German society when, in July 1933, the Reich Ministry decreed that all public employees had to give the salute. From this point onwards, the greeting became a marker for both loyalty and disobedience; for the 'chosen' volk, and those deselected from society - prison inmates and Jews were forbidden from using the salute.

Picture 40: Origin of the Roman Salute? The Oath of Horatii (1786) by Jacques-Louis David

Up until December 22nd, 1942, when it was discontinued by Congress in an amendment to the *Flag Code*, every child in an American school pledged their allegiance to the flag of the United States by raising and extending the right arm and hand to neck height. This demonstration of allegiance was popularised long before the Nazis began using it, by an American man called Francis Bellamy. Bellamy, a New York Baptist, wrote the original version of the U.S. Pledge of Allegiance and, along with his colleague - James B. Upham - created the Pledge of Allegiance flag salute in 1892 to commemorate the 400th year anniversary of Christopher Columbus arriving in the New World. Driven in part by marketing for the firm at which he worked and part by patriotism, the *Bellamy Salute* (as it was known) became a practiced ritual across the schools of America. Unfortunately, it was identical to, what would become, the Nazi salute. In the 1930's pressure began to build within America to abandon the salute because of its confusing similarity to both Nazi and Fascist ritual. However, there was also pressure within America, particularly from isolationists, to retain it. Ultimately, once Germany declared war on America most arguments ceased. Congress, supported by President Roosevelt, amended the Flag Code, which stipulated that only a 'hand over the heart' gesture should be used from that point onwards.

Picture 41: Connecticut school children pledging allegiance before World War Two

Picture 42: American school children using the Bellamy Salute as they pledge their allegiance to the flag

AFTERWORD

It would fill me with enormous pleasure to imagine that someone out there had found an element of history within the pages of this book that they had not known before. The pleasure would be deepened if that person had found said element of history just a little bit surprising. Perhaps surprising enough to desire to discover more.

With the rise of right-wing populism in a number of countries and a return to the kind of pre-war insular nationalism that helped tear the world apart in 1939, it behoves us all to take an interest in our collective past. When American private school students today feel comfortable enough to almost unanimously (almost) raise their arms in Nazi salute for a school photograph, it seems that it is time for reflection. I don't suppose for a second that these students were giving the Bellamy Salute. When countries of Europe prefer to leave refugees from war-torn neighbours floundering in the sea than take them in, it may be time to remember how the world dealt with the refugee crises after both world wars. When a demagoguery, the likes of which we have rarely seen in democracies since World War Two, enjoys an acceptance within the mainstream body politick, perhaps it is best that we take time to look backwards. Of course, I would not consider for a second that this small book holds any secrets for a successful future, however, I DO consider it of the utmost importance that my students understand our history – particularly those elements of it that seem to 'disappear' over time. It is by studying these 'disappearing' atoms of history that remembering begins.

This is my answer to the students who ask the question, "Why do we have to study the Nazis, again?".

Remember.

PICTURES

Note: *All efforts have been made to find the correct attribution for pictures contained herein. Any issues will gladly be resolved with all deliberate speed.*

Front cover:
Swastika key fob manufactured by Coca Cola 1927.
Attribution:
Photo credit: Fresh On The Net on Visualhunt.com / CC BY

Back cover:
Elephant Gate with swastika symbol at the entrance to the old Carlsberg factory in Copenhagen
Attribution:
Troels Dejgaard Hansen from Copenhagen, Denmark [CC BY-SA 2.0 (https://creativecommons.org/licenses/by-sa/2.0)], via Wikimedia Commons

Picture 1:
Hitler's euthanasia directive
Attribution:
Marcel [Public domain], from Wikimedia Commons

Picture 2:
Karl Brandt on Trial at Nuremberg
Attribution:
Public Domain

Picture 3: Indiana Eugenics Law Marker
Attribution:
Gbauer8946 [CC BY-SA 3.0 (https://creativecommons.org/licenses/by-sa/3.0)], from Wikimedia Commons

Picture 4: Heinrich Gross

Attribution:
Jurgen1303 [CC BY-SA 4.0
(https://creativecommons.org/licenses/by-sa/4.0)], from
Wikimedia Commons

Picture 5: Aktion T4 Memorial
Attribution:
Photo credit: naotakem on Visual Hunt / CC BY

Picture 6: Visit if Hitler and Goebbels to the UFA
Attribution:
Bundesarchiv, Bild 183-1990-1002-500 / CC-BY-SA 3.0 [CC
BY-SA 3.0 de (https://creativecommons.org/licenses/by-
sa/3.0/de/deed.en)]

Picture 7: William Dudley Pelley
Attribution:
Harris & Ewing [Public domain], via Wikimedia Commons

Picture 8: German American Bund insignia/flag
Attribution:
Paloeser [CC0], from Wikimedia Commons

Picture 9: German American Bund parade in New York
Attribution:
New York World-Telegram and the Sun staff photographer
[Public domain], via Wikimedia Commons

Picture 10: Fritz Kuhn
Attribution:
Unknown author [Public domain], via Wikimedia Commons

Picture 11: Carl Laemmle & the White Front Theatre
Attribution:
CharmaineZoe's Marvelous Melange on VisualHunt / CC BY

Picture 12: Independent Moving Pictures Co. logo

Attribution:
Internet Archive Book Images on Visual Hunt / No known
copyright restrictions

Picture 13: Poster for *All Quiet on the Western Front*
Attribution:
Corporate author/original rights holder: Universal Pictures
[Public domain], via Wikimedia Commons

Picture 14: German translation of Remarque's *All Quiet on the
Western Front*
Attribution:
H.-P.Haack [CC BY 3.0
(https://creativecommons.org/licenses/by/3.0)], via
Wikimedia Commons

Picture 15: MS St. Louis surrounded by smaller vessels in the
port of Hamburg
Attribution:
https://encyclopedia.ushmm.org/content/en/photo/the-st-
louis-in-the-port-of-hamburg. Sourced from Wiki Commons

Picture 16: Carl Laemmle with his son Carl Jr. & daughter
Rosabelle
Attribution:
Library of Congress, Prints & Photographs Division,
[reproduction number, e.g., LC-B2-1234]. Publisher: L Bain
News Service. Now held in George Grantham Bain Collection

Picture 17: Das perfide Albion
Attribution:
By Alfred Geiser, German propaganda pamphlet from World
War One. Original source of file unknown

Picture 18: German propaganda piece blaming Chamberlain
for the war. Published in "Die Wehrmacht 1940.
Attribution:

Picture 19: SS 'Black Book'
Attribution:
Reichssicherheitshauptamt of German Government 1940
[Public domain or Public domain], via Wikimedia Commons

Picture 20: St Lawrence Radar Tower, Isle of Wight
Attribution:
Ben Gamble / RAF St.Lawrence
https://upload.wikimedia.org/wikipedia/commons/4/4f/RAF
St.Lawrence-_geograph.org.uk_-_89021.jpg

Picture 21: The swastika flag of the Nazi Party
Attribution: Unknown

Picture 22: America's second female pilot, Matilde E. Moisant, 1912
Attribution:
Unknown author [Public domain], via Wikimedia Commons

Picture 23: Nosecone of Spirit of St. Louis
Attribution:
San Diego Air & Space Museum Archives on Visualhunt.com /
No known copyright restrictions

Picture 24: Heinrich Schleimann
Attribution:
Unknown author [Public domain], via Wikimedia Commons

Picture 25: Present day Washington County Court House, Ohio
Attribution:
Kindly permitted to use by photographer John Jackson

Picture 26: The Marinebrigade Ehrhardt during the Kapp Putsch
Attribution:
Bundesarchiv, Bild 146-1971-091-20 / CC-BY-SA 3.0

Picture 27: Swastika key fob manufactured by Coca Cola 1927.
Attribution:
Fresh On The Net on Visualhunt.com / CC BY

Picture 28: Finnish Air Force plane during World War Two
Attribution:
Unknown author [Public domain], via Wikimedia Commons

Picture 29: Insignia if the Finnish Air Force Karelia Air Command. Designed by Olof Eriksson,   approved by the President of Finland in 1957
Attribution:
Overall design by Olof Eriksson, main emblem by Akseli Gallén-Kallela. [Public domain], via Wikimedia Commons

Picture 30: Kipling cover
Attribution:
Charlie Brewer on Visual hunt / CC BY-SA

Picture 31: Inside of Rudyard Kipling's 1909 book, Actions and Reactions
Attribution:
Unknown

Picture 32: The present-day flag of Kuna Yala
Attribution:
S/V Moonrise [GFDL (http://www.gnu.org/copyleft/fdl.html), CC-BY-SA-3.0 (http://creativecommons.org/licenses/by-sa/3.0/) or CC BY-SA 2.5 (https://creativecommons.org/licenses/by-sa/2.5)], via Wikimedia Commons

Picture 33: Röhm and Hitler
Attribution:
Bundesarchiv, Bild 146-1982-159-22A / CC-BY-SA 3.0 [CC BY-SA 3.0 de (https://creativecommons.org/licenses/by-sa/3.0/de/deed.en)]

Picture 34: Kurheim Hanselbauer Hotel
Attribution:
Teilzeittroll [CC BY-SA 3.0 (https://creativecommons.org/licenses/by-sa/3.0)], from Wikimedia Commons

Picture 35: The Blutfahne riding with Hitler in 1935
Attribution:
Charles Russell Collection, NARA. [Public domain], via Wikimedia Commons

Picture 36: Hitler and Röhm
Attribution:
Bundesarchiv, Bild 102-14081 / CC-BY-SA [CC BY-SA 3.0 de (https://creativecommons.org/licenses/by-sa/3.0/de/deed.en)]

Picture 37: Hitler's Zweites Buch
Attribution:
Deutsche Verlags-Anstalt [Public domain], via Wikimedia Commons

Picture 38: Dedication in Mein Kampf to newlyweds
Attribution:
Markus Wolter [CC BY-SA 4.0 (https://creativecommons.org/licenses/by-sa/4.0)], from Wikimedia Commons

Picture 39: The Red Cross ID document of Adolf Eichmann aka Ricardo Klement
Attribution:

The photographer who took Eichmann's photo used in the passport is unknown. [Publicdomain], via Wikimedia Commons

Picture 40: Adolf Eichmann on trial in Israel
Attribution:
Huntington Theatre Company on Visualhunt.com / CC BY

Picture 41: The Oath of Horatii (1786) by Jacques-Louis David
Attribution:
Anne-Louis Girodet de Roussy-Trioson [Public domain]

Picture 42: Connecticut schoolchildren giving the Bellamy Salute while pledging allegiance
Attribution:
Library of Congress Prints and Photographs Division Washington, D.C. 20540 http://hdl.loc.gov/loc.pnp/pp.print

Picture 43: Schoolchildren in New York giving the Bellamy Salute
Attribution:
New-York tribune [Public domain], via Wikimedia Commons

BIBLIOGRAPHY

Bailey, B. (1993) *The Kid from Hoboken: An Autobiography*. US: Circus Lithographic Prepress

BBC History, *Hitler Plans the Invasion of Britain*. Available at: http://www.bbc.co.uk/history/events/hitler_plans_the_in vasion_of_britain (Accessed: June 2018)

Berenbaum, M. (2018) *T4 Program, Nazi Policy*. Available at: https://www.britannica.com/event/T4-Program (Accessed: September 2018)

Black, E. (2012) *War Against the Weak: Eugenics and America's Campaign to Create a Master Race*. Washington: Dialog Press

Boissoneault, L. (2017) *The Man Who Brought the Swastika to Germany, and How the Nazis Stole It*. Available at: https://www.smithsonianmag.com/history/man-who-brought-swastika-germany-and-how-nazis-stole-it-180962812 (Accessed: August 2018)

Carr, Steven Alan. (2001) *Hollywood and Anti-Semitism: A Cultural History up to World War Two*. UK: Cambridge University Press

Doherty, T. (2009) *Hollywood Censor: Joseph I. Breen and the Production Code of America*. USA: Columbia University Press

Ellis, J. (2014) *How Blackpool Helped Britain Win the War*. Available at: https://www.blackpoolgazette.co.uk/news/how-blackpool-helped-britain-win-the-war-1-6376036 (Accessed: October: 2018)

Evans, Susan E. (2004) *Forgotten Crimes: The Holocaust and People with Disabilities.* Chicago: Ivan R. Dee.

Forczyk, R. (2016) *We March Against England: Operation Sealion, 1940-41.* UK: Osprey Publishing

Ford, H. (1920-1922) *The International Jew: The World's Foremost Problem.* Abridged version published by Martino Fine Books (2011)

Friedlander, H. (1995) *The Origins of Nazi Genocide: From Euthanasia to the Final Solution.* North Carolina: University of North Carolina Press.

Friedmann, J. (2010) *Flowers for the Führer in Landsberg Prison.* Available at: http://www.spiegel.de/international/germany/adolf-hitlers-time-in-jail-flowers-for-the-fuehrer-in-landsberg-prison-a-702159.html (Accessed: June 2018)

Gabler, N. (1989) *An Empire of Their Own: How the Jews Invented Hollywood.* Anchor
German Propaganda Archive. Available at: https://research.calvin.edu/german-propaganda-archive (Accessed: 2018)

Goebbels, J. (19th January 1929). Diary Entry. Available at: https://spartacus-educational.com/GERsa.htm (Accessed: July 2018)

Hall, A. (2017) *Battle to save 'Night of the Long Knives' hotel where Hitler turned on Brownshirts' leader Ernst Röhm - the only man standing in his way to absolute power - in deadly 1934 purge.* Available at: https://www.dailymail.co.uk/news/article-

4993210/Battle-save-Hitler-s-Night-Long-Knives-hotel.html (Accessed: August 2018)

Hancock, E. *"Only the Real, the True, the Masculine Held Its Value": Ernst Röhm, Masculinity, and Male Homosexuality.* Journal of the History of Sexuality, Vol. 8, No. 4 (April 1998) pp. 616-641. University of Texas Press

Handicapped: Victims of the Nazi Era. Available at: https://www.ushmm.org/learn/students/learning-materials-and-resources/mentally-and-physically-handicapped-victims-of-the-nazi-era/euthanasia-killings (Accessed: July 2018).

Hawkins, E. & Browne, R. (2017) *Does Finland need its swastikas?* Available at: (https://yle.fi/uutiset/osasto/news/does_finland_need_its_swastikas/9865204) (Accessed: August 2018)

Heiden, K. (1938) *Hitler: A Biography.* England. Constable & Co., Ltd

Heller, S. (2008) *The Swastika: Symbol Beyond Redemption?* USA: Allworth Press

Hiro, Dilip. (2013) *Iran Under the Ayatollahs.* UK. Routledge & Kegan Paul Inc., p.296

Hitler, A. (1922) Available at: http://www.hitler.org/speeches/09-18-22.html (Accessed October 2018)

Hitler, A. (1939) Available at: http://hitler.org/speeches/04-01-39.html (Accessed October 2018)

Hitler, A. (1939) *Mein Kampf.* London: Hurst and Blackett Ltd.

Hitler, A. (1941-1944) *Hitler's Table Talk, 1941-1944: His Private Conversations.* Translated by Norman Cameron and R. H. Stevens. Preface by Hugh Trevor-Roper. GB. Enigma Books.

Hoberman, J. (2009) *The Moguls and the Dictators: Hollywood and the Coming of World War II.* Available at https://www.filmcomment.com/article/the-moguls-and-the-dictators-hollywood-and-the-coming-of-world-war-ii/ (Accessed November 2018)

Unknown Author. *Introduction to Nazi Euthanasia.* Available at: http://www.holocaustresearchproject.org/euthan/index.html (Accessed: September: 2018)

Johnson, D. (2003) *Revealed: the amazing story behind Hitler's second book.* Available at: https://www.telegraph.co.uk/culture/books/3603289/Revealed-the-amazing-story-behind-Hitlers-second-book.html (Accessed: January 2018)

Kaelber, L. (2015) *"Am Spiegelgrund".* Available at: https://www.uvm.edu/~lkaelber/children/amspiegelgrundwien/amspiegelgrundwien.html (Accessed: October 2018)

Kershaw, Ian (2001) *The "Hitler Myth": Image and Reality in the Third Reich.* Oxford University Press.

Mansky, J. (2017) *This Hollywood Titan Foresaw the Horrors of Nazi Germany. Available at:* https://www.smithsonianmag.com/arts-culture/this-hollywood-titan-foresaw-horrors-nazi-germany-180961828/ (Accessed November 2018)

Nuremberg Military Tribunals. (October 1946-April 1949) *Trials of War Criminals Before the Nuernberg Military Tribunals, Vol I*. Superintendent of Documents, US Government Printing Office

Nuremberg Military Tribunals. (October 1946-April 1949) *Trials of War Criminals Before the Nuernberg Military Tribunals, Vol II*. Superintendent of Documents, US Government Printing Office

Plöckinger, O. (2016) *Adolf Hitler's "Mein Kampf", 1922-1945*. Germany. De Gruyter Oldenbourg

Purvis, A. (2000) *Suffer the Children*. Available at: http://content.time.com/time/world/article/0,8599,20504 69,00.html (Accessed: August 2018)

Rabinbach, A. (2016) *Struggles with Mein Kampf*. Available at: https://www.the-tls.co.uk/articles/public/struggle-with-reality/ Accessed: July 2018)

Read, C. (1997) *The Evolution of Adolf Hitler's Weltanschauung: A Critical Study of His Rhetoric*. Massey University.

Rising, D. (2010) *Hitler's cushy prison life in the 1920's revealed*. Available at: https://www.independent.co.uk/news/world/europe/hitle rs-cushy-prison-life-in-the-1920s-revealed-2008754.html (Accessed: June 2018)

Ross, Steven J. (2004) *Confessions of a Nazi Spy: Warner Bros., Anti-Fascism and the Politicisation of Hollywood*. Available at:

https://searchworks.stanford.edu/view/7931846
(Accessed July 2018)

Ross, Steven J. (2017) *Hitler in Los Angeles: How Jews Foiled Nazi Plots Against Hollywood and America*. USA: Bloomsbury.

Ross, Steven J. (2017) *The Hollywood Nazi who Spied for America*. Available at:
https://www.washingtonpost.com/news/made-by-history/wp/2017/10/25/the-hollywood-nazi-who-spied-for-america/?noredirect=on&utm_term=.a490fc6384ed
(Accessed: September 2018)

Rothman, Lily. (2018) *Operation Finale Shows the Capture of Nazi Adolf Eichmann. But What Happened at His Trial Changed History, Too*. Available at:
http://time.com/5377670/operation-finale-adolf-eichmann-trial/ (Accessed: September 2018)

Russell, S. (2017) *John Capes, In WWII When His Submarine Sank He Swam 170 feet To The Surface and Swam 5 miles To Shore*. Available at:
https://www.warhistoryonline.com/world-war-ii/submarine-sank.html (Accessed: September 2018)

Schmidt, H. D. (1953) *The Idea and Slogan of "Perfidious Albion."* Journal of the History of Ideas 14, no. 4, 604-16.
doi:10.2307/2707704.

Schnitkter, H. (2011) *The Church and Nazi Germany: Opposition, Acquiescence and Collaboration II*. Available at:
https://www.catholicnewsagency.com/column/the-church-and-nazi-germany-opposition-acquiescence-and-collaboration-ii-1657 (Accessed: June 2018)

Searle, A. (2017) *Churchill's Last Wartime Secret: The 1941 German Raid Airbrushed from History.* UK: Pen and Sword

Sherwood, H. (2012) *Adolf Eichmann's capture, as told by the Mossad, in Israel exhibition.* Available at https://www.theguardian.com/world/2012/feb/15/adolf-eichmann-exhibition-tel-aviv (Accessed: June 2018)

Smith III, Edward C. (2015) *Nazi Propaganda and the 1930 Berlin Film Premiere of "All Quiet on the Western Front".* World Academy of Science, Engineering and Technology International Journal of Humanities and Social Sciences. Vol: 9, No: 5, 2015

Stockton, R. (2016) *How American Eugenics Programs Inspired the Nazis.* Available at: https://allthatsinteresting.com/american-eugenics (Accessed: August 2018)

Stockton, R. (2018) *Aktion T4, The Nazi Program That Slaughtered 300,000 Disabled People.* Available at: https://allthatsinteresting.com/aktion-t4-program (Accessed: June 2018).

T4 - Memorial and Information Centre for the Victims of the Nazi Euthanasia Programme. Available at: https://www.visitberlin.de/en/t4-memorial-and-information-centre-victims-nazi-euthanasia-programme (Accessed: August 2018)

The Motion Picture Production Code. Available at: https://www.asu.edu/courses/fms200s/total-readings/MotionPictureProductionCode.pdf (Accessed: November 2018)

Tran, M. (2009) *Hitler's plan to turn Blackpool into a Nazi resort come to light.* Available at: https://www.theguardian.com/uk/2009/feb/23/hitler-blackpool-resort-plans (Accessed: October 2018)

Unknown author. (1938). *Riot in New York at German Ship Bremen: Swastika Torn Down and Thrown into Hudson River.* Taken from https://forward.com/culture/380130/from-the-archives-riot-in-new-york-at-german-ship-bremen-swastika-torn-down/ (Accessed: September 2018)

Unknown author. (2010) *Britain Stands Alone.* Available at: http://www.historyplace.com/worldwar2/defeat/britain-alone.html (Accessed: July 2018)

Unknown author. (2017) *Did Hitler want to make resort his playground?* Available at: https://www.blackpoolgazette.co.uk/news/did-hitler-want-to-make-resort-his-playground-1-8408968 (Accessed: October 2018)

Unknown Author. *From Ideology to Racism: Hitler's Mein Kampf.* Available at: http://web.nli.org.il/sites/NLI/English/collections/personalsites/Israel-Germany/Weimar-Republic/Pages/Mein-Kampf.aspx (Accessed: July 2018)

Unknown author. *Hitler's Dark Vision for the UK.* Available at: https://www.history.co.uk/shows/ww2-treasure-hunters/articles/hitlers-plans-for-the-uk (Accessed: September 2018)

Unknown author. *Hitler's views on the British Empire to 1924.* Available at: http://www.bennionkearny.com/hitler-views-on-britain-and-british-empire/ (Accessed November 2018)

Urwand, B. (2013) *Did Hitler run Hollywood?* Available at: https://www.telegraph.co.uk/history/world-war-two/10343881/Did-Hitler-run-Hollywood.html (Accessed July 2018)

Urwand, B. (2013) *The Chilling History of How Hollywood Helped Hitler.* Available at: https://www.hollywoodreporter.com/news/how-hollywood-helped-hitler-595684 (Accessed July 2018)

Woronzoff, E. (2018) *Double-agents, Movie Stars, Studio Moguls, and 'Hitler in Los Angeles'.* Available at: https://www.popmatters.com/hitler-los-angeles-steven-j-ross-2532169325.html (Accessed: September 2018)

OTHER WORKS BY ELLIOTT L. WATSON, PATRICK O'SHAUGHNESSY, AND VERSUS HISTORY

Amazon Bestseller:
33 Easy Ways to Improve Your History Essays:

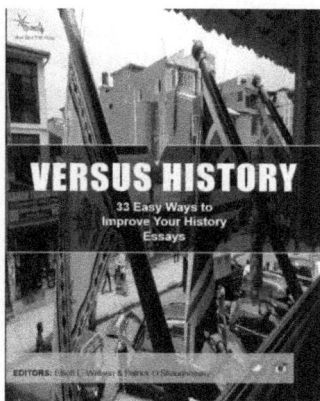

Lord Durham and the Canada Question:

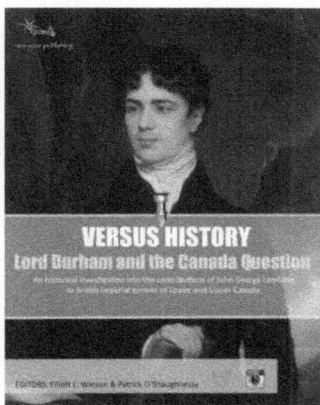

Don't forget our leading weekly **Versus History Podcast**, available from wherever you download your podcasts.

Websites
www.versushistory.com

Twitter:
@VersusHistory
@thelibrarian6

Instagram:
versushistory

www.ingramcontent.com/pod-product-compliance
Lightning Source LLC
Chambersburg PA
CBHW030105070426
42448CB00037B/975